Ten Men, a "Flying Boxcar," and a War

Ten Men, a "Flying Boxcar," and a War

A Journal of B-24 Crew 313, 1944 to 1945

Emmett G. (Mac) MacKenzie

iUniverse, Inc.
New York Lincoln Shanghai

Ten Men, a "Flying Boxcar," and a War
A Journal of B-24 Crew 313, 1944 to 1945

Copyright © 2005 by Emmett G. MacKenzie

All rights reserved. No part of this book may be used or reproduced by any means, graphic, electronic, or mechanical, including photocopying, recording, taping or by any information storage retrieval system without the written permission of the publisher except in the case of brief quotations embodied in critical articles and reviews.

iUniverse books may be ordered through booksellers or by contacting:

iUniverse
2021 Pine Lake Road, Suite 100
Lincoln, NE 68512
www.iuniverse.com
1-800-Authors (1-800-288-4677)

ISBN: 0-595-34738-X

Printed in the United States of America

Dedication

By Emmett (Mac) MacKenzie

This book is dedicated to the members of B-24 Crew No. 313 and their families. I could not have served with a finer group of men during World War Two. Not only were they dedicated to help bring the war to its inevitable conclusion, but also they were dedicated to working together to insure the safety and lives of each other.

This book is also dedicated to the men of the 376th Heavy Bombardment Group and to the men of the 514th Squadron, who were quartered in San Pangrazio, Italy during the years 1943 to 1945.

Crew No. 313 Roster

1st Lieutenant Roy Hatem, pilot
2nd Lieutenant William Anclam, copilot
2nd Lieutenant Michael Oczkus, navigator
Warrant Officer Guy Bretilotte
Technical Sergeant Paul O'Steen, flight engineer
Technical Sergeant Lou Birnbaum, radio operator
Staff Sergeant Jim Snell, top turret gunner
Staff Sergeant Byron Hunsicker, tail gunner
Staff Sergeant Andre' Duval, belly gunner
Staff Sergeant Emmett MacKenzie, nose gunner

Contents

Preface ix
Thumbnail Sketch of Crew No. 313 xv
CHAPTER 1   The B-24: Design and Development 1
CHAPTER 2   The Forerunners and the Early Days: July 1942 5
CHAPTER 3   Coming Together and Training as a Crew: June 1944 14
CHAPTER 4   Destination Italy: October 5–11, 1944 20
CHAPTER 5   The Reality of War: Late October 1944 26
CHAPTER 6   Life on the Ground Between Missions: October 1944 38
CHAPTER 7   Routine and Some Non-Routine Practices: November 1944 42
CHAPTER 8   Varied Missions: December 2–15, 1944 58
CHAPTER 9   The Worst of Times: December 17–29, 1944 70
CHAPTER 10   A Quiet Time for Crew 313: January 1945 90
CHAPTER 11   Missions Increase: February 1945 99
CHAPTER 12   Memories and Reflections: March 1945 119
CHAPTER 13   Foggia, Italy: April to May 1945 145
CHAPTER 14   Heading for Home: June 1945 153
Epilogue 161

Definitions 165
Bibliography 167
Crew Biographies 169

Preface

By Emmett (Mac) MacKenzie

Forty-seven years had elapsed since I was discharged from the Army Air Force and I had gone on to get my B.A. in education and a MBS in Math and Science. Along the way, I married Pauline, raised a family, and taught high school math until my retirement. Then one morning in January of 1992, I received a phone call from a person whose voice I had not heard for many years. "This is Jim. Do you remember who I am?" I recognized him immediately as Jim Snell.

"I could never forget your voice," I told him.

He also said that he had been in contact with Roy Hatem, our pilot; Bill Anclam, our co-pilot; and Paul O'Steen, our flight engineer; but he didn't know the whereabouts of Mike Oczkus, our navigator; Lou Birnbaum, our radio operator; Andy Duval, our belly gunner; or Byron Hunsicker, our tail gunner or even if they were still alive. As we ended our conversation, Jim said that our Air Force Group, the 376th Heavy Bombardment Group Veterans Association (HBGVA) was having a reunion at Ft. Walton Beach, Florida in early September 1992 and suggested that it would be great if our crewmembers could get together there. This conversation changed the focus of my life.

After almost five decades of nary a passing thought on these matters, memories of the crew's time together during Word War Two came rushing back to me. I knew what I wanted to do. I would attempt to make contacts with each crewman. With the help of a friend, I was able to find all but one of the missing men, Lou Birnbaum.

In the summer of 1992, I decided to visit both Paul O'Steen and Mike Oczkus. Paul picked me up in his car at the Oakland airport and then drove us to Mike's home in San Rafael, California. Our excitement as we rang Mike's doorbell was met with his gracious greeting: "You guys weren't supposed to be here until tomorrow!" He hesitated momentarily and said, "Well, since you guys are here, you might as well stay here tonight." It was great reminder of Mike's dry sense of humor. After supper, Mike showed us six pages of memories he had written by hand.

One morning during this visit to Paul at his home in Oregold, California, located near the southern entry to Yosemite National Park, the phone rang. Out of the blue, it was the sole member of the crew whom we had not been able to contact, Lou Birnbaum. He said that Jim Snell had contacted him too, so he decided to call Paul. It wasn't long after these encounters that the other member began to call each other on a regular basis.

Only Andy, Jim, Lou, Roy, and I attended the first reunion. After talking to each other for hours, I went home and pondered what to do next. Then it came to me. Using Mike's six handwritten pages, I began writing my first newsletter for the entire crew, the <u>Crew No. 313 Newsletter</u>. I was hopeful that the crewmembers would participate by providing me with more autobiographies and stories. By July 1994, I completed the eleventh and it turned out to be the last newsletter and mailed it to the remaining crewmembers and to the wives of the four members who had died by then. I realized that that job was done and I began work on the next. Those newsletters became the spark that ultimately led to the development of this book.

What follows is a collection of stories, or more precisely, a journal of events related to our crew's experiences while flying during World War Two in a B-24, or as some airmen affectionately called it, the flying boxcar.

I have tried to keep the book's contents as factual as possible while writing from memory of the related experiences of various crewmembers. After each mission, the company clerk completed a report, called a "Form 5 Report." I saved my copies and they were invaluable prompts for my recollections. Of course, memory can play tricks, especially on a would-be historical writer. But, to the best of my ability, this is the truth of my crew's experiences.

Airman's Individual Flight Record

Acknowledgements
By Emmett (Mac) MacKenzie

In August 1992 at the time of the 49th reunion of the 376th Heavy Bombardment Group Veterans Association, (HBGVA) all ten members of the original B-24 bomber crew, Crew No. 313, were still alive. Their voices can be heard in these pages. As of the date of this publication, only three remain: Bill Anclam, Lou Birnbaum, and Andy Duval. Hopefully, through our stories, we crewmembers can share our experiences with our future generations.

I have had the very special privilege to meet with every member of our crew, with the exception of Guy, and to reminisce about our times together. My time was well spent listening to these men and their recollections. But the added bonus was the opportunity to become personally re-acquainted with them after nearly a half-century of silence.

A special thanks goes to Michael Ozckus, our navigator, who wrote out longhand over 38 pages of very valuable recollections of our days together between July 1944 and July 1945. Secondly, I wish to recognize Paul O'Steen, our crew's flight engineer, for his priceless contribution, a copy of his diary. Paul's diary not only enabled me to confirm certain events and facts, it also preserved the first-person accounts and the feel of the events as they happened. For that reason, I've included appropriate excerpts after the mission summaries as Paul wrote them (with the addition of some minor copy edits). Thirdly, I wish to thank Roy Hatem, our pilot, for the hours he spent with me relating stories and events. Using our Form 5 Flight Records, I was able to confirm and sequence the dates of our missions and sorties. To Jim Snell, our top turret gunner, I will be ever grateful for his ability to verify many of the events as well as providing me with many stories.

I wish to thank the following members, and the wives of deceased members who supplied autobiographies, biographies, pictures, and stories for this history of Crew No. 113: Bill Anclam, copilot; Dorothy Hunsicker, wife of our tail gunner, Byron; Andre Duval, our belly gunner; Lou Birnbaum, our radio operator; Charlene Osteen, Paul's wife; Dorothy Oczkus, Mike's wife (now deceased); and Guy Bretilotte, our bombardier. Without their contributions, this chronicle would not have been possible. Each person has contributed in their own way to this history of our crew.

Included in this history is a story, gratefully accepted, that relates to the early days of the 376th Heavy Bombardment Group. Charles Hobbes, a pilot in the 512th Squadron, and his son, Kim, are the contributors. Charles' story depicts the hazardous life of one crew during the 1943 North African campaign.

A hearty thanks to the people who helped me with computers and software, formatting, and research including Ruben Aga, Tom Henchal, Nick Ferriola, Dave Lange, James Lynch, John Redfield, and Julie Stiche; and to Jean Peterson, who helped with proofreading and advice. To Michael Orange, who determined the best format and took on the job of managing the production and printing of this, my first effort to write a book, I extend my thanks and gratitude.

Finally, I wish to thank my wife, Pauline MacKenzie, for her valuable literary incites that so improved the manuscript.

Thumbnail Sketch of Crew No. 313

(Detailed biographies are at the end of the book)

By Emmett (Mac) MacKenzie

Roy Hatem (1919–2002), 1st Lt.: Roy's home was New York City. He was a gong-ho young man in his early years, stocky and strong, which was to serve him well in the future. He joined the Army National Guard and gave his age as 18 and was assigned to the 69th Regiment. Later, he joined the New York Police Force and remained with the organization until, being unable to withstand the urge to serve his country, he join the Army Air Force. He was 26 when our crew was formed, and he was relentless in his pursuit to master all the technical details required to be a B-24 pilot. As a married man, he eagerly applied himself to the ground and flight courses, and his strong will and determination to return to his wife, Dorothy, and his yet unborn son was a built-in insurance policy that he would see that he and his crewmembers would return home intact. In short, he was a perfectionist. He demanded much of himself and of those who served under him. Roy had all the physical qualities that served him well when piloting the not-so-easy-to-fly B-24.

A lighter side of Roy was his love for singing over the intercom with Lou Birnbaum, the radio operator, after he successfully made it through another mission. Some of their favorites were "Lilly Marlene," "I'm a Yankee Doodle Dandy," and "I Want a Paper Doll that I Can Call My Own."

William Anclam (1921–), 2nd Lt.: Prior to working at the Parker Pen Company in Janesville, Wisconsin, Bill, too, was bitten by the military bug. He wanted to become a fighter pilot even though he was married man. His wife, June, didn't object. Having finished all the required ground and flight training courses, he was ready to fly a fighter plane, but as luck would have it, a call was sent out by the Army Air Force to have men who had trained to become fighter pilots to serve as copilots in B-24s. He was not a happy warrior, but took what fate had handed him and became a good B-24 copilot at the age of 24.

Bill was also a strong and ruggedly built blond-haired man; just the type needed to help fly a B-24. In general, he was a happy-go-lucky guy, always ready to play a good prank when the opportunity presented itself. He was well liked by the other officers as well as the enlisted men.

Michael Ozkcus (1923–1993), 2nd Lt.: Mike claimed the Bronx as his hometown. Slim and good-looking as a young man, Mike was good at mathematics in high school. When it became his turn to serve, he chose to become a navigator, and, like Roy Hatem, he was a perfectionist at his chosen trade. To the crew's knowledge, he never made an egregious mistake in his calculations. Often following a mission, he would do a self-evaluation of that day's navigational tasks. A serious person by nature, he also loved to have a good time when not on duty. Latter in life, he became a great storyteller and writer. But best of all, early in our crew's history, he was the enlisted men's advocate at the age of 22.

Guy Bretilotte (1922–1994), Warrant Officer: Guy was from a small town in Iowa. He was an introvert who kept to himself much of the time. However, as the crew's bombardier, he took his work seriously. He studied maps and charts in preparation for each mission and he also knew well the job requirements of an ordinance and armament specialist. He knew that he probably would be responsible for the accidental death of some civilians, which was an agonizing thought for Guy. At the age of 22, he would carry this sense of moral responsibility.

Paul O'Steen (1921–1993), Tech. Sgt.: Paul hailed from California. He was a sandy-haired, six-foot, medium-built, young man with piercing blue eyes, behind which was a powerful intellect. He learned his trade as an aircraft mechanic and flight engineer at Seymour Johnson Air Base in North Carolina. Paul was the replacement for the first flight engineer who left the crew shortly after the crew began training at Charleston Air Force base in Charleston, South Carolina. Paul was a highly qualified flight engineer. In flight, he was a no-nonsense man dedicated to his job. He also knew that he as much as the pilots would be responsible for the lives of all the crewmembers. Off duty, however, he also knew how to enjoy himself and did so.

Paul was the only crewmember who kept a record of the missions he had flown. Little did he know the value of his diary in later years as he noted his flight experiences along with the targets that had been hit.

Lou Birnbaum (1925–), Tech Sgt.: Lou grew up in Massachusetts. He was a well-built young man about 5–9 in height. Lou was a bit shy and was an unassuming young man of 21 years who believed wholeheartedly in physical fitness. He was the only member of the crew with light red, curly hair. After graduating from high school, he worked for his father, a furniture builder and fabricator. Lou was talented dancer who frequently visited the local ballrooms with his girlfriend, Anne. He not only loved to dance but also loved to sing the current pop songs.

His position on the crew was that of the radio operator. He often said that he didn't do much, but whenever Roy wanted to communicate with squadron headquarters or the squadron flight leader, Lou was always ready, be it a verbal or coded message. His alternate responsibility was that of a waist gunner.

Jim Snell (1919–1998), Staff Sgt.: Jim's hometown was Columbia, Missouri. His demeanor was that of a self-assured and confident mature man. After high school, he began training for his life's work as a mechanical engineer, starting as a gopher for the local power and light company. He was a considerate, gentle, and soft-spoken individual who brought his experience and know-how. His position was that of the top turret gunner. Jim was the only married enlisted man on the crew. Because of his ripe old age of 24, he was known as the "Old Man."

Byron Hunsicker (1924–1993), Staff Sgt. Brian had been a star, high school athlete at Willoughby, Ohio. A well-built, stocky young man with a mass of thick dark hair and eyebrows under which resided a pair of intelligent and penetrating dark eyes, Byron was 20 when he joined the crew. His specialty was armament. As a gunner, he was the best and he performed his job with cool assurance. He manned the tail turret position. He, too, was carefree and liked to have a good time, a carry-over from his high school days. He left behind his girl friend, Delores, who later became his wife.

Andre Duval (1926–), Staff Sgt.: Andy, as we called him, was the youngest of the crew at only 19. His youth disguised his intelligence, as he was a fast learner and he possessed a sharp mind. Although a quiet person, one could see him taking in all the experiences that unfolded before him. He had a girlfriend back home whose name was Jeannette, whom he later he married. Since he was also the smallest of the crew, he was just the right size for the ball turret position.

Emmett MacKenzie (1923–), Staff Sgt.: Mac was a six-foot, brown-curly-haired, rather serious-minded young man of 22. He had worked a year after graduating from high school and earned the $300 he needed to attend the University of Colorado in the fall of 1942. (Tuition was $45, board was $12 per month at the Student Union building, and a room in a private home was $11 per month.) He had just finished the second quarter in Engineering College when, as an Air Force Reservist; he was called to active duty.

On home leave prior to joining the crew, he took flying lessons in a Piper Cub. He loved it when the flight instructor showed him how to recover from a spin. The instructor pulled up the nose of the plane and stalled it out. Then, after he let the nose drop down and go into a nerve-wracking spin, he recovered control by applying opposite rudder and pushing the stick all the way forward.

Mac was a bit of a loner. Making true friendships didn't come easily to him. Maybe this was true of other members of our crew, as all our backgrounds were quite different. But when faced with projects that benefited the enlisted men or confronted with life-threatening situations, he pitched right in and did his part.

★   ★   ★

Although our backgrounds were quite different, we all worked together to fulfill the mission before us, and to do the best job possible, individually and collectively, to bring the war to its inevitable end. Paramount for each of us was to protect each other for the common good.

1

The B-24: Design and Development

By Emmett (Mac) MacKenzie

David Davis: Aeronautical Designer and Engineer

David Davis was a self-taught aeronautical designer and engineer. What follows is an excerpt from the book by General Dynamics, *Liberator* that describes the designer, the design problem, and the result:

> [David Davis] envisioned a plane having a wing with very special characteristics. In fact he designed and patented the "Fluid Foil" wing in 1931. Davis had solved the problem of "air resistance" never solved previously by other designers since the time of the Wright brothers. He constructed a wing foil, which could be driven through a fluid with particular attention being given to the profile of the foil in its front to rear section. It was designed for high-speed performance, 300 mph.
>
> Not until 1939 when the U.S. Government realized that the B-17 could not meet the needs of a heavy bomber did Davis have a chance to propose the incorporation of his wing design into an entirely new and radical approach to a heavy bomber aircraft design

In 1938, General "Hap" Arnold, chief of Army Air Corps, was responsible for the evolving air arm branch of the Army. He was among the most foresighted and aggressive proponents of air power in the military. He made known his need for a very special aircraft to supersede the B-17 and laid out the specifications and invited the aircraft industry participation. The new bomber must exceed 300 mph, have a cruising range of 3000 miles, and fly at a ceiling of 35,000 feet.

At about the same time David Davis and Donald Douglas, a Glenn L. Martin Chief Engineer joined together to form the Davis-Douglas Aircraft Corp. They presented their plans to Washington but got nowhere in their discussions. Only Rueben Fleet, president of Consolidated, believed in the Davis wing design. Disillusioned, Davis severed ties with Douglas and gave the wing design to Consolidated asking only for the royalties of foreign sales. Later he hooked up with Billy Mitchell, a controversial, aggressive military air tactician, pilot, and leader for whom the B-25 Mitchell medium bomber was eventually named.

Davis followed his wing design with another innovation, the "Variable Pitch" propeller, which was depended on hydraulic fluid control rather than on a purely mechanical control.

B-24 Design Specifications

The B-24 had so many firsts to its credit that they must be enumerated. It was the first bomber to have:

- Tricycle hydraulic operated landing gear, a system that allowed a shorter landing distance.
- Fuselage mounted under the new 110 ft. "Davis Wing," bomb bay doors that slid up the sides of the fuselage on tracks creating far less drag the plane's surface when the doors were open.
- Hydraulic operated landing gear which were stored during flight in carved out areas in the second and third engine nacelles and behind the engines.

- Neoprene fuel storage tanks contained in its wing cavities.
- Fuel transfer system that could selectively supply or cut off fuel to any one or more engines and at the same time serve as a device to help distribute and balance the weight of the plane while in flight.
- The capability to carry a maximum load of 8,000 pounds of bombs.
- The power to exceed 300 mph with slight variations in the latter two specifications depending on the production model.
- Cruising speed of 215 mph.

The J Model had the Following Specifications:
- Length of 67" 2."
- Wing area of 1,048 square feet, a wingspan of 110 ft.
- Gross weight of 65,000 lbs, a capacity to carry 8,000 pounds of bombs.
- Top speed of 290 mph; cruising speed of 215 mph.
- Cruising range of 2,100 miles,
- Service ceiling of 28,000 ft.
- Equipped with four Pratt Whitney R-1830-65 engines."

The B-24J models were produced in greater numbers than any other model. In fact, the Liberator was destined to become the most pugnacious workhorse; and in general was the greatest all-purpose bomber of that era. It was affectionately known as the "flying boxcar."

Incongruously, the B-24 had the most beautiful and graceful wing of any plane aloft. It was used as a high altitude bomber, a submarine hunter, a low-level dive-bomber if need be, and a transport, and a carrier of VIPs.

The bomb bay area of the plane was designed to include two bomb bays, each of which contained two bomb racks, one on each side of the catwalk. The catwalk was a structural walkway that connected the two bomb bays with the flight deck bulkhead and the plane's waist section bulkhead. Each bomb rack contained five bomb hangers for a total of 20 bomb hangers. The maximum load was 8,000 lbs, regardless of the configuration of the hangers used.

A total of 18,190 variations of the B-24 were built, more that any other aircraft ever built. Now there are probably only three planes left. One B-24J that the 513th Bomb Squadron in Italy flew is on display at Air Force Museum at the Wright Patterson air base in Dayton, OH. The Confederate Air Force owns the second, a B-24A, and the third is a composite that has been reconstructed as a B-24J and owned by the Collings Foundation. The latter two planes may be seen at air shows around the country.

2

The Forerunners and the Early Days: July 1942

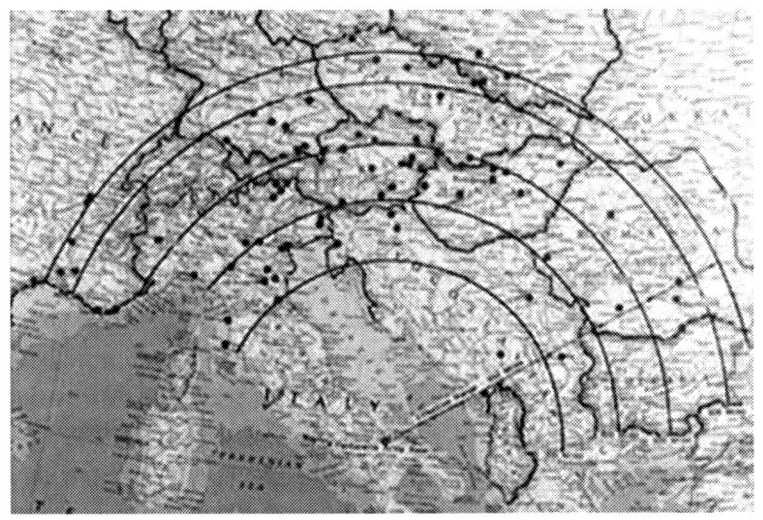

Range of the bombing missions for Crew 313

By Emmett (Mac) MacKenzie

The Halpro Group and the African Campaign

This story dates back to the time when 23 newly built B-24Ds were formed into an organized military group for the United States under the directive of General 'Hap' Arnold. It became the forerunner of what would become the United States Army Air Corps and the model for other bomb groups including ours. According to the *Liberator*, "He thought it wise to form small striking forces that could begin hitting the enemy sooner rather than later. It would require a year to develop a full-fledged fighting force." One of these striking forces was called the provisional Halpro Group, which was comprised of a 213-man task force, formed and led by Col. Halverson.

The Halpro Group was trained in the United States and was supposedly destined to attack the Japanese Empire from China, a destination never realized. This group was also called the Liberandos. As fate would have it, the Liberandos Group was ordered to begin bombing the Italian fleet in the Mediterranean Sea from bases in Lydda, Palestine and later from Algeria, Africa.

The Southern European War Theater had its beginnings in Northern African. The German tank commander, General Erwin Rommel, led the African campaign of 1942. Rommel's goal was to conquer the whole north rim of Africa. He had taken Tunisia on the far west and was intent on moving through Algeria and Alexandria, Egypt, jumping the Suez Canal, and ultimately threatening the Middle East oil supply. Rommel's campaign goal changed forever the original mission of the Halpro Group Liberandos.

This is the setting for the following story that began with the crew of the B-24 named the Wild Wolf. The time was during this campaign of 1943 that Charles Hobbs and his crew flew their 50 missions out of Africa. The following story was typical in many respects for that time and the experiences of these early crews. I include this story here because it provides important historical insights into the organization and mission strategy that later affected all of us in Crew No. 313.

The Story Tellers

It wasn't until the reunion at Charleston, South Carolina in 1996 that I had the opportunity meet and speak to this very interesting pilot, Charles Hobbs, and his son, Kim. Charles had originally told me the story at the previous reunion in 1995. The story centers around the life of one Eddie Huddleston, the tail gunner on Charles's B-24, assigned to the 513th Squadron. I was fortunate once again to have been seated at the table with both Charles and Kim at the noon luncheon of the 376th Heavy Bombardment Group and I took the opportunity to bring up the story and life of Eddie.

This story had its origin at the time when Kim was 14 years old. Charles had taken Kim to visit Eddie at his home in Hardy, Arkansas. To say the least, Kim was very impressed with Eddie and his exploits while a member of his father's crew. After Eddie's death in 1972, Kim obtained Eddie's personal diary from Eddie's wife in 1995 and made a home videotape of Eddie's life while he was a member of the crew. On my request during that year's reunion, Kim sent me the tape. It was an intriguing and informative video of Eddie's military life in the early forties. The following is one of the stories.

The Tale of a Tail Gunner Who Wasn't There
By Kim Hobbs and Emmett (Mac) MacKenzie

Charles Hobbs and his crew had been awarded the Distinguished Flying Cross (DFC) in recognition of the contributions made in the raid on the Ploesti Oil Refineries in July 1943, as were all crews who flew the mission. However, Eddie Huddleston was not eligible nor would he ever receive a DFC for that mission because he was supposedly in the hospital recovering from a leg wound caused by a 37mm cannon shell that had passed through his left leg during the previous mission. Eddie had been confined in an earthen hospital in Benghazi, Libya called the Dug-Out, the floor of which was a couple of feet beneath the surface of the ground. At best, the hospital was a makeshift structure covered with tenting material, complete with attending doctors, nurses, and medics. But Eddie would not be confined long and soon would be out flying with his crew again and any other crew that needed an expert gunner.

Eddie's life began in De Kalb, Missouri where he was born in 1922. He grew up in the same town, loved shooting guns, graduated from high school, and enrolled at St. Joseph Junior College in Missouri. But at the age of 20, he decided to join the Army Air Corps. After he completed gunnery school at Harlington, Texas, he ultimately became a member of Charles' crew. In addition to being an excellent gunner, he was a great observer and recorder of his surroundings and of human nature. He had a gift for summarizing in a few well selected and descriptive words what he observed and felt, all of which he entered in a pocket diary that he always carried with him. As an example, he described the 513th Squadron's short-term move from Berka 11, Libya to Enfidazille near Tunis, Tunisia in the following manner: "The field is a cow pasture and the country is so flat that even a Tumble Bug didn't have to work hard."

The Wild Wolf and her crew arrived and were based in Benghazi, Libya in May 1943 and were assigned to the newly created group, the 376th Heavy Bombardment Group (HBG) of the 9th Air Force under the command of General Uzal Ent. The crew flew more than 25 missions from Benghazi between May and late August of 1943. After his 5th mission, Eddie had received the Air Medal, which was customary for all flying personnel. Prior to July 16, the crew had flown missions over Sicily, Italy, and Greece without a serious mishap. The exception was the mission on June 17th over Messina, Italy. The Germans were prepared, having increased their firepower to well over 200 guns, which would be aimed at the attacking B-24s.

Of the mission, Eddie said, "The anti-aircraft fire was so thick it was like fog, I couldn't see the next formation of planes [behind me]. I got a splattering of it. It was good a thing that I had on Air Force glasses or my eyes would have been shot out. As it was, the flak knocked out both lenses; but it was slowed up enough by the steel rims so that it just cut my eyelids a little. The rest of my face looked like it went through a meat grinder." Because of this injury, Eddie was awarded his first Purple Heart.

The heart of Eddie's story took place on July 16, 1943, the crew's 18th mission. "We were going after a German airfield that was chuck full of planes and men," he wrote. "The mission target for this day was Bari, Italy. It was the coldest mission I had ever flown. Half way across the [Mediterranean Sea], my heated suit went haywire. Coincidently, it was just one day earlier that the true age of the tail gunner on a sister crew had been discovered. He had run away from home, joined the Air Corps, and had made his way into combat without anyone having discovered his age. The Commanding Officer found out through the War Department that he was only 14 years old and told him that he could return home or he could continue to fly. It was his choice. Hell, he is still here and we are going on the mission today."

Unknown to Eddie at the time, he was going to become the recipient of an oak leaf cluster to add to his first Purple Heart, and receive the DFC for this day's work. As the 513th Squadron approached the Initial Point (initial point of target heading or IP), Charles turned the Wild Wolf on the pre-established IP and made the bomb run. Lt. Walker, the bombardier, dropped the bomb load while 21,000 feet over the German airfield. Not much anti-aircraft fire was encountered and the crew felt a sense of relief as they peeled off and headed home. But death and destruction was lurking behind a large cloud formation waiting to pounce on the squadron.

As Eddie described it, "Suddenly, Lt. Tagnasian, the navigator, shouted over the intercom, 'Here comes the Herman Goering's Hot Shots!' About 40 yellow-nosed FW-190s, fresh from the Russian front, flew out of a cloudbank. This is the first time that they ever jumped us. They hit us hard and fast despite everything we could put up against them."

Eddie's plane was the lead plane in the last box-element of the formation. He said, "I saw the chutes of the men who had bailed out of their planes passing under us. Both of the wing planes were shot down—the left wing plane carrying down with it the crew that included the 14-year-old gunner. Next it was our turn. An FW-190 charged head-on into my position and sprayed the plane with 37mm and 50cal. machinegun fire. It was as if their wings were on fire shooting those machine guns. It was just like shooting from the hip for me because I didn't have time to aim, as this guy was coming in shooting so thick and fast." Eddie returned fire and was able to shoot down the German fighter when it was only about 35 yards away. As Eddie said, "This guy must have wanted to pay off the mortgage on his folks' family farm. He just kept coming and I just kept throwing lead at him."

In the engagement, Eddie's turret was shot out of commission, his oxygen system was gone, and he had received a 37mm hole in his left leg from the fighter pilot that he had shot down seconds before. "It was a good thing that the temperature was intensely cold or I would have bled to death. I took the cord from my intercom headset and made a tourniquet. It stopped my leg from bleeding and the cold made the blood clot. Because the tail of our plane was so badly shot up and filled with holes, my intercom had been knocked out during the last 30 minutes. One of the plane's engines was out and the rest of the plane was in such bad shape, I thought the order might have been given to bail out."

Prior to this mission, neither Eddie nor Perry, his friend the waist gunner, ever wore chutes. "Crawling out of the turret, I saw the other [waist] gunner so scared stiff that he couldn't move. He was standing near the camera hatch with his chute on. I had been so damned busy, I didn't have time to get scared. But because the rest of the plane was so badly shot up and everything was in such a mess, I tried to find my chute and put it on. Perry came back and scooted over toward me to get a look at my leg. When I saw him looking at me with that possum-eating grin, I damned near passed out with relief. Schultz, the engineer, the papa of our crew, had come back to fix some cables and he doctored my leg with some sulfa powder. The Martin top turret gunner, Owens, had been shot with a direct burst of 37mm fire and was blown out of his turret. He was in a bad way. So they gave him all the morphine and I took the sulfa tablets. After a long five-hour trip back to the base, I finally got some medical attention. The top turret gunner, who was with me in the ambulance, died on the way to the hospital."

Eddie's leg had time to mend and heal from July 16 until July 31. The crew, and especially his buddy, Perry, who was like a brother to him, kept in touch with Eddie. Shortly after Eddie was hospitalized, Perry told Eddie that their crew, along with many other crews, was practicing some very special low-level raids on simulated targets over the desert. Perry certainly thought it must be something big and promised to keep Eddie posted as to when it was to come off. On the night before August 1, Perry learned that the crew had been training for the raid on a place called Ploesti, Romania. Both Eddie and Perry knew that there was a need for experienced gunners and Eddie knew that he was a damned good one. Eddie said, "They didn't want to have to go with a 'green' man," so the two of them conspired to get Eddie out of the hospital.

Perry got Eddie to the Wild Wolf early in the morning on the day of the Ploesti raid at about 5:30. There was no mention as to how it was done. The mission was to be a long one, taking 14:20 hours. The Wild Wolf flew over the narrowest part of the Mediterranean Sea, over the coast of Greece, the southeastern tip of Yugoslavia, the northwestern tip of Bulgaria, and finally to Ploesti, Romania. It was a very demanding, physically draining, and emotional mission. "We missed the target and caught hell from coming in on the wrong side." Eddie said. "We were lucky to get back. I ran out of ammo when we were hit by fighters and had to fake it. It was a good thing that the Germans decided to go home."

Eddie and Perry did the paperwork trick and Eddie was dutifully restored to his bed in the dugout hospital.

On March 1, 1944, Eddie received orders to return to the States having completed 50 missions (345 hours and 45 minutes) on February 22. By this time, Eddie had added five oak leaf clusters to his Air Medal, received the Purple Heart and an oak leaf cluster to go with it, and received the DFC for shooting down the FW-190 German fighter. However, Eddie never was to receive the DFC for his flight over

Ploesti because his name was not listed on the Ploesti mission roster for the 513th Squadron. Officially, he was never there! Such was the life and times of one Eddie Huddleston, the inquisitive, innovative, dedicated, and self-confident gunner.

The B-24 "Tidal Wave" Raid Over Ploesti, Romania

Ploesti, Romania was a major complex of oil companies. The Nazis bought it from a multi-national conglomerate of oil companies in the mid 1930s. By the time the U.S. entered the war, Ploesti was the primary source of fuel for the German war machine. The book, *Liberandos*, states, "A study of the Ploesti complex indicated some unique features. Large and small refineries surrounded the city of Ploesti. Most of the production capacity was confined to five major units immediately around or near the edge of the city, and two others, one eighteen miles northwest at the town of Campina, and one five miles south of the village of Brazi."

It was crucial that the U.S. and its Allies disrupt and destroy the production capabilities. The mission was known as the "Tidal Wave." To get a mental picture of Ploesti, think of it as a hexagon, standing on one of the six vertices. Starting with the top vertex and moving clockwise, the "Waves" and their refinery targets were as follows: R-1 (Campina, approx 20 miles south of Ploesti), White-1 (5 miles east of Ploesti), White-II (on the Northeast side), White-III (southeast side), White-IV (southeast edge/vertex), and White-V (southwest vertex/edge), and Brazi. The Campina and Brazi were separate raids and not technically a part of the Tidal Wave missions.

The original plan of attack was top secret and called for five groups to hit the target simultaneously. The newly formed 389th was to bomb Campina and the 376th Bomb Group was to hit White-I. The 93rd Bomb Group, Flight A was to hit White-II and Flight B was to fly over the city and hit the target White-III. The 98th Bomb Group would fly over the southwest side of the city and bomb White-IV and the 44th Bomb Group Flight A would bomb White-V while the Flight B hit Brazi.

The 376th's first initial turning point (IP) was Floresti, Romania, and then on a wide arc, to turn southeast to place the group directly over W-1. However, the Commanding Officer of the 376th and leader of all the groups was flying as an observer when the best laid plans began to unravel. Afraid that his group was about to over-fly the first IP, he took command and ordered the group to turn right, over a town named Targoviste, Romania, thinking it was the first IP. Using ground-observation-navigation, he thought that the 376th was approaching the correct IP, Floresti. Actually, he had turned the group approximately 20 miles short of the designated IP and was heading in a southeast direction <u>away</u> from Ploesti. The lead navigator protested but was over ridden.

Major Norman Appold was the squadron leader for the 514th Squadron. According to Appold, his navigator, Bull Reading, called on the intercom and protested the turn. "We're not to the I.P. yet!" Appold decided to break radio silence and called 'Wrong Turn' several times, but nevertheless turned his formation into a trail position behind the forward elements of the 376th. The group commander discovered his mistake a few minutes later, and ordered his group to turn north and head toward Ploesti in the face of the other oncoming squadrons. They were coming in from the north and on the same low-level attack altitude as the 376th. It was a completely chaotic situation. Everyone was confused, including the Germans. German intelligence had already picked up the approaching B-24 groups after they had passed over the Adriatic Sea and were following them as they had approached their target in Romania. Because of this error, the 376th group had to dodge not only the other groups and squadrons, but also the German anti-aircraft gunners.

The cost of this mission was the loss of over 50% of the attacking B-24s.

3

Coming Together and Training as a Crew: June 1944

By Emmett (Mac) MacKenzie

The Crew

We came together in late June 1944, at Westover Air Base in Massachusetts. Inside the base theater the new pilot's names were read out loud by a base officer who was in charge of the program. Each pilot had a list of names of men who were assigned to his crew. Then the name of each airman was also read out loud and each man was told to go to the area where each pilot checked off the names of his new crew. Roy introduced himself and told us that we would be traveling to Charleston, South Carolina for further training. After that, we all began to talk and introduce ourselves.

This was the second time that I had been assigned to a crew in six weeks. Having returned from home on a month's furlough, I had contracted food poisoning the day I was supposed to ship out with the first crew. I had a bad headache so on the way to the base debarkation point; I decided to stop off at the area infirmary for a couple of aspirin. The medics on duty took my temperature, which was 106 degrees, and immediately sent for an ambulance to take me to the base hospital where I was confined for a week. On reflection, I was glad that I didn't go with the first crew because I sensed that something was missing in the crewmembers. Maybe it was the drive, stamina, or will to make it through the war.

Arriving at Charleston South Carolina, on approximately June 2, 1943, our crew trained until September 12th having been assigned to the 113 AAF Base Unit D. I have no memory of the type of training we received initially, but it must have been some kind of ground training that occupied the crew's time during the month of June. However, we flew a total of 79:40 minutes practicing our individual specialties from August 2nd through September 12th.

Our crew was designated as an overseas replacement crew #13 and assigned to a B-24 bomber.

The Chow Line

During the month of June, I had a very vivid recollection of the food served at the "mess hall" at least three or four times a week. Unknown to me, the menu on those days called for goat or horsemeat to be served. My stomach was in no mood to experiment with this questionable menu. It seemed as though the cooks took exceptional delight in preparing for the noon day menu so that they could see expression on the Airmen's" faces as they came face to face with main course to be served for the day. At first I wondered what kind of meat was being served. I had never seen anything like it before. Someone said, "Well, soldier this is horsemeat. You had better get used to eating goat and horse meat." After several encounters with either kind of meat, it didn't take long for my sense of smell to zero-in on the menu in the days ahead—be it horsemeat or goat. I could smell the goat meat a block away from the mess hall. It was bah-bad. And in the case of horsemeat, it is red and stringy. Not only was its appearance repulsive, it was tough and tasteless, let alone almost impossible to chew. The sight of and the smell of these offerings was enough to cause me to quickly bypass by these forms of protein. Thereafter when the smell of horse or goat meat waffled through the air, I would immediately head for the PX and get a hamburger. Thank God for the food bar and the sight of real beef!

Cross Training

Each of the enlisted men had trained at various schools specializing in gunnery, radio communication, air mechanics, and armament. Five of us were assigned to a 50cal. gun position, that is, the nose, top, belly, and tail turrets as well as waist window positions. We spent many hours firing at tow targets. Then Roy, our pilot, assigned each of the officers to an alternate task position: Bill trained to become the first pilot; Mike had enough responsibility just being the navigator but could double as the bombardier. Guy, the bombardier, took on the job of the first aid officer. Guy continued to practice taking over the control of the plane via the Norden Bomb Sight after Roy lined him up on the Initial Position (IP) to follow for the bomb run. The crucial aspect of being the bombardier was to make sure that the plane was precisely lined up on the target when striving for the maximize effect of hitting the target squarely and precisely. On practice runs, Guy released bags of white powder, simulating bombs aimed at the ground target.

But one time when Guy released a dummy bomb, it landed outside of the outer rim of the target. Those of us who saw where it landed laughed. But for Roy, it was no laughing matter. He told Guy that we would practice the bombing drops until he could hit the target squarely on the center circle. That admonishment did the trick. Shortly thereafter, he did hit the target. Paul and Lou busied themselves perfecting their skills as flight engineer and radio operator but could double as waste gunners. Byron cross-trained as the bomb armament specialist; Jim trained as the assistant flight engineer, and I trained to be the assistant radio operator. Roy was a great believer in cross training, which was of great value to our survival.

Lost Over the Bahamas

Roy related to me the following event in one of our numerous conversations. On this flight, Mike was to sharpen his skill as our navigator.

Our mission was to fly out over the Bahamas, circle and return to base. Another purpose for the crew was to learn how to work together. But on this mission, we got lost over an area called the Bermuda Triangle. It was here that our plane encountered a powerful storm front that swept in over our plane. Mike was working from his last know position and trying to extrapolate the plane's present course and heading. There was no sun. It was just clouds and rain. Roy did not want to let ground control know that we were lost and kept "radio silence" hoping Mike could get a bearing on our position. Failing that, Roy told Lou to break silence and radio the base for the necessary heading to get us back to Charleston. We did not communicate with base control again until we landed without incident, much to the surprise of Base Operations. Two other crews also had been out of touch with base operations, but we were the first to land safely and to report in, much to our relief.

Segregation Southern Style

Another incident that I remember vividly was the bus ride from the base to Charleston. Noticing that many of the seats in the middle of the bus were empty, I wondered down the isle and immediately became aware of my first experience with segregation. It was a sobering experience for me. The Blacks were forced to sit in the back of the bus so when they got on the bus, there was not question about where they were heading. It seemed very unfair to treat them in that manner. Another reminder of the South's early treatment of the "blacks" in the south and particularly Charleston was the sight of a large marble platform that stood eight or ten feet above the street. Underneath the platform was the area where individuals and families were forced to stand until they were called on to go up on the platform. The slave auction block was located near Battery Front that looked toward Fort Sumter.

End of training in Charleston

All of our training flights had been flown in B-24 Js. This was because there were more B-24 J's built than any other model. But now the training had come to an end. Between September 12 and 27, 1944, we must have had a few days to our selves followed by a party for the crew before we left Charleston. Then the wives of Roy, Dorothy; Bill, June; and Jim, Dorothy left to return to their homes.

Mitchell Air Force Base: The Staging Area, Garden City and Long Island, New York

Taking a slow train from Charleston to Long Island, New York, we must have arrived somewhere around the 29th of September. Jim and Roy seem to remember that we stayed about a week at Mitchell Army Air Force (AAF) Base, where we were quartered in Section U, the staging area of the 110th Unit. Obviously the days that followed were taken up by Roy, Bill, and Paul studying the flight characteristics of the B-24L that we were to fly across the Atlantic. The record indicates that on October 3, 1944, we flew orientation and practice flights for a total of 3 hours and 55 minutes. A lucky omen for our plane designation number was the number 313 and we were also the 13th replacement crew. We were also lucky to get passes in the evening night, so it was New York City here we come!

Prepping the Troops and Indoctrination and Shots

Finally, the crew received indoctrinations pertaining to our military and social behavior while in Italy in addition to practicing "bailout" and "rescue" procedures if we should have to bailout over the Atlantic. We were all given ample shots of vaccines to ward off any "bugs" that might present themselves. Besides being equipped with wrist watches and a 45 caliber hand guns, we were given stuff that implied we might be going to a base in Africa—how about mosquito netting, a fishing lines, lures and hooks; and lastly a 14 inch machete knife for cutting through a jungle? Never could figure that one out, as we were destined for Italy!

Having completed our training, we received a three-day pass and then went to Mitchell Air Force Base on Long Island, New York. Mike said that a few days at Mitchell were great because the base was just twenty miles from New York City. Brooklyn was my hometown."

The Empire State Building

Mac: The enlisted men decided to tour New York City. One place we had to see and experience was the Empire State Building—about 110 stories high. We took the elevator to the observation deck passing through floors 12 and 14. There was no 13th floor. Thirteen was supposed to be a taboo (an unlucky) number. But it wasn't for our crew. Getting back to our tour of the city. We were there in the evenings experiencing the "Big Apple" and all that it had to offer. Having been told the crew was leaving on the 5th, I called home on the 4th to wish my mother a happy birthday but couldn't tell her where we were headed.

Before leaving Mitchell field, the supply depot loaded our plane down with blankets, canned foods. The Red Cross gave us two or three boxes of best know classical books to read. It was as if we were going to be gone a long time. Blankets, food, and reading material, who could ask for anything more?

Before leave New York, Roy decided to fly circles around the Empire State building. The feeling was that we were going to slip and slide into the building on that bright and sunny morning. What a sensation! In Roy's mind, it was like saluting a farewell to city and country. After all, New York was Roy's hometown. But the stunt did exhibit Roy's skill at handling a B-24, which later was to be called on with the help of Bill to save our crew over the Yugoslavian Alps.

4

Destination Italy: October 5–11, 1944

By Mike Ozkcus and Emmett (Mac) MacKenzie

The first leg of our flight began on October 5th at midmorning. Our destination was Bangor, Maine where we were to stay three days because of bad weather. Bangor was a very dreary place: no sun, only clouds and rain. On the fourth day, the 9th, we flew off to Gander Bay, Newfoundland where we stayed for three days—again a case of bad weather. This was to be our jumping off point from the North American continent. Gander was one of those typical Lend Lease Canadian air bases from which American planes either went to England or Italy.

It was here that the enlisted men had a little adventure of their own. On the second day there, the enlisted men, including Mac, decided to go boating across a rather large shallow lake in an old flat bottom rowboat. The outing was to relieve the boredom and provide some needed exercise. All six enlisted men went and all were needed in that boat. After rowing out into the middle of the lake, it began to rain and the wind blew furiously. The harder we rowed to get back to the boat dock, the further the boat was blown away from the dock. Before we knew it, the wind had blown our boat to the opposite side of the lake into the marshes where we had to leave it. Wet, cold, and soaked, we trudged at least a mile along the marsh shoreline. Luckily, we were spotted by a couple of locals who came out in a motorboat and took us back to the dock. We were most grateful for the rescue.

While at Gander, we met our first reality of war. At a briefing of our flight to San Miguel in the Azores Islands, we were informed that a B-24 had cracked up on take-off on the runway. It was on fire and the entire crew was lost. Ground control considered canceling the flights but the weather was so good that it had to be a "go." When we took off for the Azores on the 12th, the last sight we saw of the land was the B-24 burning in the night.

San Miguel was approximately 1,650 miles from Gander Bay and 1,150 miles from the Rock of Gibraltar, the most westerly end of the Mediterranean Sea. This flight would be the longest we had to fly and we were all a little bit apprehensive about finding a small island in the middle of the Atlantic. The flight took 7 hours and 15 minutes. Technically, the B-24 was designed to fly 3,000 miles without refueling.

Late in the afternoon, we could see the Azores straight ahead. It was here that we had our first encounter with fate in what might be called the "Toggle Switch Incident." With the Azores in sight, Roy called Mike out of the nose compartment and asked him to come up onto the flight deck. On the deck, he received a lot of left-handed complements and "well done's" because it was our first ocean flight and it was very successful. In the midst of all this, Paul yelled out that there was no oil pressure in #3 or #4 engine. And then, almost at the same time, all four engines had no oil pressure registering on the instrument gauges. Roy told Bill to feather the engines (align the cutting edge of the propellers blades with the length of the plane) and he immediately got on the intercom system and ordered the entire crew to take up positions for an "at-sea-ditching." Mike had removed and left his "Mae West" life preserver jacket and parachute harness in the nose of the plane. No rabbit ever moved faster to get back to the nose and get on his Mae West.

When he returned to the flight deck, everything was fine as if nothing had happened. The Azores was just ahead of us, only now we were just above the water but all four engines were operating on full power. Roy explained that someone had accidentally turned off the master switch. The master switch works just like the ignition in a car. Turn on the key and all electricity becomes active including all the instruments. In our B-24 the master switch does the same thing. The only difference is that instead of a key, there's a toggle switch located at the rear of the control box. Nothing further was said, but I assumed someone had hit the switch with his elbow. There was nothing wrong with the engines. It was just that the electricity to the instruments had been turned off. A crewmember discovered the error. It is a credit to the pilot, copilot, and the crew chief that they caught the mistake. Otherwise we would have ditched a perfectly good and operational B-24 with probably some loss of life. We made it to the Azores in spite of ourselves.

We did not stay there long, only one night. It was a very poor and miserable place that time had forgotten.

San Miguel, the Loneliest Dot in the Atlantic Ocean

San Miguel Island did have its rough and isolated beauty. In the late afternoon after settling into the barrack lodgings on a steep hillside overlooking the base, Andy and Mac decided to take a little stroll. They walked back down the path, climbed over several rock fence walls, crossed rocky pastures, and ended up sitting on the last rock wall that overlooked the Atlantic Ocean in an easterly direction. As the sun set, calm and beautiful, they sat there isolated from the rest of the world and the war. After they returned to camp, they learned that they should not have gone sightseeing across the pastures and stone fences because of the rats and the diseases that they carried. They nested in the rock fences.

After chow, we all went to the base movie. When the movie was over, there were small dim lights around the canteen area, but as we began walking up the narrow and steep pathway toward our lodgings, there were no lights or moon to illuminate our way. We were all stumbling along trying to stay on an invisible trail. It was pitch black all around us except for the heavens. They really put on a show for us; an unparalleled spellbinding display of the constellations. It was as if we had been giving a special showing of creation.

Gioyia, Italy: Flying Across Northern Africa the Mediterranean Sea and on to Italy

On the 13th, we began our fourth leg, flying from the Azores to Marrakech, Morocco in 6 hours and 40 minutes. On the 14th, the fifth leg of our flight, we refueled and then took off for Tunis, Tunisia. On October 15th, we flew from Tunis to Gioyia, Italy. It took 3 hours and 30 minutes to complete the sixth and final leg of our flight. The only other experience that was noteworthy was our encounter with the U, S. Navy. As we crossed the Mediterranean Sea, we flew too close to a Navy ship. We were given a warning shot to "bug off." No one flies over U.S. warships! This was our first and last encounter with the Navy's "friendly fire."

By 4:00 P.M. we had touched down in Gioyia, Italy (pronounced Joya), a little town nestled in a picturesque valley with broad, rolling hills. Down the middle of the valley was the landing strip made up of thousands of perforated steel planks, which were hooked together to form a mesh, 3,000 feet long or more. The city was a distribution center for the Army Air Force. Everyone was eager to get out of the plane and head for the mess hall. It had been a long flight from Marrakech.

On arrival, we had to give up our plane. Our crew was assigned a truck to transport us the 62 miles to San Pangrazio, the home of the 514th Bomb Squadron of the 376th Heavy Bombardment Group

(HBG). (San Pangrazio was about 50 miles southeast of Toranto and its bay, and about 20 miles from Lecci on the southwestern coast of the Adriatic Sea.) There we would be assigned a different B-24. Mac drew the first watch to guard the plane that brought us safely across the Atlantic. The scene from the airstrip across the wide green valley had a quiet serenity. Off in the distance in the twilight and on a hillside stood a lonely and small stone building or tomb that reflected the grandeur that once was Romania with its leaders such as Julius Caesar.

While in the mess hall at Gioyia, several fighter pilots from Northern Italian bases talked to us about the food. They were hungering for K-Rations. They said the food in their camp was not edible and they supplemented their diet with K-Rations. It just so happened that our plane was loaded with them. No one knew why. Possibly they served as useful ballast. We realized we might find ourselves in the same predicament so Roy rounded up a couple of Jeeps and drove out to our plane and loaded up 30 cases of K-Rations, two boxes of books, and a pile of blankets. It was all we could carry. We transferred all of our loot to the truck and Roy drove us from Gioyia to San Pangrazio. We arrived in the late afternoon on the 15th and split up loot among the crewmembers. After that, whenever the food at our mess hall was inedible, we would take a stack of bread and toast ourselves some cheese sandwiches.

The truck we used to get to the 514th Bomb Squadron was a standard, olive drab Army truck equipped with wooden-slat seats along the sides of the truck bed, a heavy green canvas cover and an open rear end. Riding in the back was uncomfortable, hot, and dusty. The highways were not paved, just dirt roads. Only the streets of some of the towns that we passed through were paved with brick. We passed through Massatra, Taranto, Gioyia, Sava, Manduria, and finally San Pangrazio. While passing through Gioyia or Sava, the degree of poverty was striking. The street was paved with rough cobblestones, just wide enough for our truck to pass through. On each side of the street was a long row of single-story stone buildings that were separated from each other by animal shelter stalls, also made of stone. The entrance at the front of each stall was an open archway. The animals, mostly goats, were confined to the interior by a crudely made stick gate held together with wire. Undoubtedly the goats provided the children with milk to drink. These areas had a bad smell. Imagine having to live next door to a stable! The living quarters were probably no more than 12 feet wide and maybe 18 feet deep facing the street. The front of the impoverished looking dwellings generally contained no more than one door and one window. Poorly dressed children and adults stood before the windows or in doorways and watched us as we rumbled by in our truck. Was life for these people always so meager and harsh?

5

The Reality of War: Late October 1944

A B-24 crashes on landing

A Tragic Welcome to the 514th Squadron
By Mike Ozkcus

I remember the people of the little town of San Pangrazio in southern Italy. They were very poor because the soil was so very poor. About all they raised were grapes, wine, and olives. Their homes were made of a cheap building material called Tufa blocks, which were quarried and cut from a soft yellowish stone that hardened when exposed. As for the runway, it was made of ground-up Tufa material. In the evening, the Italian laborers would fill in the ruts and holes of the runways with this

Tufa material or dirt. In the morning after a few planes had taken off, the Tufa material and dust from the previous filled holes would be blown away and the planes that followed would try to get airborne while bouncing from one hole to another. After the planes departed, the workers would return and fill in the holes.

The 514th Heavy Bomb Squadron (HBS) had a policy of paring up the key men from a new crew on their first mission with an experienced crew. Probably all the squadrons in the 376th HBG had the same policy. For example, our pilot flew copilot for a crew that had been in combat before. At first, we were all on different planes. So, the breaks go! Our "break-in" mission was to fly to Vienna, also know as the "Big V." Vienna had more than 600 anti-aircraft guns. The crew that I flew with really had it laid on them. After this mission, I would be a seasoned veteran. We took off but I don't remember for how long or how far we flew because Headquarters aborted the mission before we could drop our bombs, probably because the weather over "Big V" was bad. We didn't have an alternate target, so we came home with our bomb bays fully loaded with eight 500-pound bombs and nearly full fuel tanks.

The first returning planes blew away the Tufa material and those that followed bounced from one hole to anther. The aborted mission did not provide enough time for the laborers to even fill in the holes. My plane landed safely, taxied to its parking strip, and turned around to face the runway just as the next plane hit one of those holes right in front of us with its nose gear. As the nose of the plane went into the ground, the tail went up into the air and then it split in two just behind and wings and blew up. I watched it all. There was no flame, just a big puff of black smoke. Like flak, you can't see the flames, just the black smoke. There is really no time for reaction to something like this, just disbelief. My first thought was, "Which member of my crew was on that plane?" I got out of the plane and ran towards the explosion. Its main force went upward. There was flesh all over the runway. I saw a hand and turned around and saw an armless and headless torso. I retched and went back to the plane where we waited for the truck to pick us up. It wasn't until I returned to my tent that I found out that none of my crew was on the plane. After that experience, we were never the same. I will never forget that scene

Amazingly, not one of the 500-pound bombs exploded. They were found about a hundred feet from the point of impact with their arming pins still intact. All this in less than ten days after we had witnessed the loss of two B-24s and twenty men, none of whom had been lost due to enemy action.

Same Tragedy from Another Point of View
By Emmett (Mac) MacKenzie

We enlisted men also witnessed this tragedy but from a distance. It was customary for incoming enlisted men to be quartered in an oblong circus tent that house two or three crews at one time. The entrance was a large opening at one end of the tent. Additionally, the opening faced the runway, which was less than a mile away. That day, I was standing at the entrance of the tent watching the B-24's land one after another in a routine manner. Then all of a sudden, a very large black cloud of smoke replaced the image of a plane. I could hardly believe what I saw. I yelled to our crewmembers to come over to see and every man in the tent went into a state of disbelief. One of the members of another crew asked our crew if we wanted to go down to the runway and get a better look. Man for man, the guys in our crew said no way are we going down to the runway and see all that carnage. We knew that to witness such a catastrophe would not be good for our psyches. Later, we saw the members of the other crew that did go down to the runway. We could see the change in their demeanor. They were jittery, frightened, and predisposed to question their fate. They would never be the same.

This account of the tragic end of a crew has come full circle 58 years later. I happened to run into two associate members of the 376th HBG at a reunion. Judy Guiterras and Doug Jolman were making inquiries about the 1944 tragedy and asked me if I knew any thing about it. I told her I was there and I gave both an early draft of this chapter my book. Judy told me that her cousin had been a member of that crew.

Doug, with whom I spoke, told me that his father was the pilot of the ill-fated crew. Both people have done extensive research into the tragedy and had been trying to bring closure to the event.

He also told me he had researched the accident and that probably the main gear tires of the plane were hit by flak At that point, the plane carrying Doug's father and crew veered off the runway, rolled into a broad ditch. The nose-wheel collapsed causing the nose to plow into the ground while the twin tails of the plane rose up vertically as if it were making a final salute. Instantly the gas tanks dumped gas on the flight-deck crew as the bombs broke loose from their moorings in the bomb bay. The bombs slashed, tore, and raced through the bulkhead, scraping and tearing metal. It was as if they sought out the lowest level of the plane. The scrapping of metal immediately ignited the 100-octane gas tanks causing the horrendous explosion. The other incoming planes and observing ground personnel saw the instant flash of fire. On Inspection, the investigating military team saw all the bombs, except for one, that had rolled across the adjoining field intact accept for the one bomb that had exploded. This tragedy would be indelibly recorded in every man's mind.

The Hard Luck Crew
By Mike Ozkcus

The dictionary defines the word "jinx" as something or someone believed to bring bad luck. In the following story, the crew itself was the jinx.

When we arrived at the 514th Squadron to start our tour of duty, there was a crew that had already flown several hard missions. They had never returned to home base in the plane assigned to them. On their very first mission as a crew, they were marked for disaster. Flying a crippled plane south over the Adriatic Sea, they headed towards the fairly large island called Vis, which was off the coast of Yugoslavia and, at the time, was held by the British. It also had a landing strip located there mainly for planes that were having trouble. The plane couldn't make it. With Vis in sight they had to ditch the plane. All the eleven crewmen survived the ditching.

When ditching a B-24, one of the procedures is to assign someone on the flight deck, usually the crew engineer, to pull a cord that released two fully inflated life rafts with oars into the water. However, on this occasion only one partially inflated life raft with no oars was released. Several men jumped into the water close to the raft, and inflated it so that it was usable before the rest of the men were allowed on board. The last man left on the plane was the photographer who was to travel with the crew for just this one trip. He stood there alone at the waist window, his head bleeding badly. At the crew's urging, he jumped into the water, and some of the men pulled him into the raft. So that made eight men in the raft with no oars. They used their hands as paddles. The remaining men in the water kicked their feet while holding onto the raft until it was their turn to replace the men on board. All were working hard to get to Vis.

As the tide came in, they seemed to get closer; but as the tide went out, it carried them further away. This ordeal lasted three days and the crewmembers had no food, no water, and were exposed to the elements, all of which sapped their waning energy. The injured man became delirious and began to push others into the water. Eventually, the men on the raft became very tired of having to climb back into the raft, which added to their own fatigue. At this point the injured man repeatedly fell out of the raft into the water. Too tired to keep pulling him back into the raft, the men just took turns holding him in the water so that he wouldn't drown. But he did die and the men just let him drift away. Shortly thereafter, the remaining men were rescued.

Later, I met the officer. He was tall, thin, and spoke with a southern accent. His crew had flown a total of four missions by then and had never made it back to base after any of them. They usually landed somewhere at one of our bases in northern Italy. As we spoke, he was very nervous and quiet—on edge. I still remember his name.

To set the stage for what happened next on the crew's fifth mission, I need to explain one of the landing procedures that is necessary before a B-24 can land safely. After the pilot lowers the nose landing gear, the crew chief has to crawl beneath the flight deck and place a pin in the nose gear to lock the wheel down and in place. After not making it back to their base for their first four missions, many of us came to the landing strip to watch this hard luck crew make it home for the first time. We watched the planes circle the field in formation. One by one, each plane peeled off from the formation, lined up with the runway, lowered the dual main wheels with the main gear hydraulic system, lowered the nose wheel gear in the same manner, and then dropped down to the ground touching the dual main wheels first, followed by the nose wheel. Gradually, each plane eased down on the locked-in-place nose wheel. When it was his turn, the luckless crew pilot made his approach and prepared to set his plane down. He was heading for a perfect landing. First the main wheels touched the ground. Everybody was cheering. And now for the touch down of the nose wheel…as he gently eased the nose of the plane down, the wheel began to recede into the wheel well! The more the weight of the plane was transferred to the nose wheel, the more the wheel receded into the wheel well. Instead of a perfect three-point landing, the plane made a two-point, dual-wheel-and-a-nose landing. The tail rose up into the air and the nose skidded down the runway. No one could possibly describe the disbelief on our faces as we watched, and yet we were looking right at it. No more cheering, only wide-open-mouth disbelief. The crew chief had forgotten to put the nose gear pin in place.

The jinx was broken at last.

I met the copilot a year later. He was flying copilot for the Air Transport Command. He was bright-eyed and bushy-tailed and his girl friend denied him nothing. We chatted for a while and parted. I never saw that crew again. The word was that the 15th Air Force sent the pilot, the copilot, and the enlisted men home, and the navigator and bombardier to the ground troops.

Enlisted Men's Jinxes
By Emmett (Mac) MacKenzie

After us enlisted men had settled down into the routine of squadron life and had flown sorties and missions for a month or so, we made some interesting observations. First, there was this one particular Army tent that the billeting personnel could not keep occupied. It seemed as though each time a crew was assigned to that tent, something would happen to them. Rumors and theories floated around to explain the empty tent—the crew's plane was shot down, they had to ditch, or the Germans, Italians, or Croats captured them. The Croats were the worst of the lot. We knew that they would immediately execute survivors. They were Yugoslavians and mostly Christians living in the northern regions of the country and were politically and philosophically tied to the Nazis.

It was not unusual to pass by the tent and see a padlock on the wooden tent door, indicating that the crew was gone, certainly due to one of these terrible fates. The door remained locked on this jinxed tent until the personal possessions of the airmen could be removed and returned to their families. Then the cycle of occupancy would begin over again. The tent was unlocked, a new crew would move in, and they'd only be seen for a short time until their untimely departure. Then the tent would again be free for the next unlucky crew.

None of our crew ever got to know these new crewmen because, for one thing, they were not there long enough. This phenomenon gave us all an eerie feeling. Finally, after several crews had disappeared in this manner, the billeting personnel stopped assigning new crews to this tent. It remained there only as a memorial to those men who had the bad luck to be assigned to it.

The second jinx was related to crews who wanted to have a "certain look of distinction," as we called it. Unwittingly before leaving the States, a few crews would decide to buy blue, yellow, or red baseball caps. They would have these caps embroidered with some kind of a design, scrambled eggs, or whatever. No question about it, these guys did have that certain look of distinction. They were quite proud of their caps because the caps set them apart from the general run-of-the-mill enlisted crews in the squadron. In a sense, the caps did set them apart from the other crews, but not for the reasons they intended. They had set themselves up for a second kind of jinx: "Thou Shall Not Wear Caps Having a Distinctive Design." We knew of other crews that worn similar caps. They had disappeared under circumstances similar to the crews that occupied the Jinxed Tent.

Finally, a day came when our crew was so intrigued by this phenomenon that, at long last, we had to take action. A matter of such a serious nature demanded action, even though the means to be employed would appear to be sporting and down right prankish. This latest of new crews had to be saved from the possession of their caps.

It was late in the afternoon on one balmy day that we hatched a plan to deflect this jinx from this innocent and naïve crew. I believe it was Paul O'Steen who came up with the plan. So off we marched up to the door of the tent that housed this elite crew. We were greeted and invited in. After we introduced ourselves and made some small talk, we zeroed right in on the real purpose of our visit.

In an off-handed manner, O'Steen said, "You know your caps are quite distinctive. No other crew in our squadron has such good looking caps."

"Oh, is that right?" said one of their smiling crewmembers.

"We got them before we left the States," said another member. "In fact, we agreed on this cap and its design so each one of us bought one."

"Well, it's just great that ten guys can agree on such a person item," Paul said.

At that point, the rest of our crew chimed in and added to this new crew's sense of pride and well-being. The next comment could have been made by anyone of us, because we all had the same idea in mind for dropping a blockbuster on this new crew. We all wanted to completely crush their egos.

"You know, I think there is something that you guys ought to know about your caps." The new crewmembers looked at us as if anticipating the confirmation of their good taste in selecting their prized possessions. Then one of them asked what we meant by that comment. "Well, you see we have been observing that there have been other new crews that have had caps similar to yours."

Pausing momentarily to heighten the effect of what he was going to say next, one of our guys said, "You know what?" followed by a short pause, "I know you won't believe this, but their stay in the squadron didn't last long!"

The anticipated response appeared immediately on their faces. A deep and thick silence fell over the conversation that could not have been cut with the sharpest of swords. Recovering momentarily from the effects of this pronouncement, one of their brave souls blurted out their crew's real concern. "What do you mean, 'they didn't last long?' What happened to them?"

With an air of concern, compassion, and ever-so-straight faces, one of our crew related the consequences of wearing the caps. "New crews wearing caps like yours disappear, never to complete their missions. In fact, they disappeared shortly after they came into the 514th Squadron. One can only guess, but they probably got shot down, had to ditch their plane in the Adriatic, or they were interned in prison camps. If they were captured by the Croats, it would be even worse."

All the while, we observed the growing terror that surfaced in their facial expressions as their minds raced to take in the magnitude of what had been said. Their eminent danger was immediately connected with the wearing of their caps! And we, the innocent observers that we were, had just struck terror in their midst with a swift and unerring thrust of a few well-selected words.

Returning to our tent, we laughed uproariously as we reflected on their frightened reactions. We had pulled off the most successful ploy of our lives, having penetrated the depths of their hearts with a few well-chosen words. A couple of days elapsed before we once again had the occasion to see member of the new crew. Gone were the ornate caps and in their place were the tried and true G.I. issued caps. The jinx had been circumvented by our noble and unselfish intervention to save this crew from an uncertain and imponderable fate.

Officer Familiarization Missions

About a week after we had arrived at the 513th Squadron, Lt Hatem, Lt. Bill Anclam, Lt. Mike Ozckus, and Warrant Officer Guy Bretilotte were assigned to fly as observers with seasoned crews on a mission/sortie

Crew 313 participated in the following missions 376th Bomb Group, Mission No. 349, October 16, 1944

Mission status:

- Target: Stekyr, Austria; St. Valentine Tank Works
- Airmen points: 2 sortie, 1 mission
- Total flight time: 7:15 hours
- Distance to target: Unknown

Aircraft statistics:

- Aircraft at takeoff: 40
- Aircraft over target: 38
- Aircraft returning to base: 4
- Aircraft diverted or forced to land: 4
- Aircraft destroyed (mech.): 1
- Aircraft missing: 1
- Aircraft damaged: 2 major, 1 minor (anti-aircraft)

Flight leaders:

- A Flight: Major Snyder & Lt. French (512th Squadron)
- B Flight: Lt. Krines
- C Flight: Lt. Upshur

Mission summary:

- Group bomb load: 243 500-lb bombs
- Bombing results: Superior
- Airmen casualties: 11 missing, 2 seriously injured
- Anti-aircraft: Heavy to moderate and accurate
- Mission commentary: Flights A and C missed the target. Flight saturated aiming point, many fires and explosions.

376th Bomb Group, Mission No. 350, October 17, 1944

Mission status:

- Target: Vienna, Austria; South Ordinance Works
- Crew points: 2 sortie, 1 mission
- Total flight time: 6:40 hours
- Distance to target: 480 miles (510 km)

Flight leaders:

- A Flight: Major George & Lt. Krines (513th Squadron)
- B Flight: Lt. Kamps

Flight box configuration:

Lt. Krines		A	
Lt. Johnson	B	C	Lt. French
Lt. Floerke		D	

Aircraft statistics:

- Aircraft at takeoff: 27
- Aircraft over target: 26
- Aircraft returned to base: 21
- Aircraft diverted or forced landing: 2
- Aircraft lost: 2 destroyed
- Aircraft damaged: 2 major, 1 (anti-aircraft), 3 minor
- Aircraft destroyed (mech.): 1
- Aircraft missing (anti-aircraft): 1

Mission summary:

- Bomb load: 206 500-lb bombs
- Bomb results: Path Finder Fix, very superior
- Airmen casualties: 4 killed, 22 missing, 2 lightly wounded
- Anti-aircraft: Heavy to intense
- Fighter escort: 50 P-38s and P-51s.

6

Life on the Ground Between Missions: October 1944

By Mike Ozkcus and Emmett (Mac) Mackenzie

We lived in a well-organized and safe camp comprised primarily of British pyramid tents and two buildings that housed the Operations and the Officer's club that were more or less solid buildings made of Tufa blocks. The tents were about ten feet square, the wooden sides were about three feet high, and the roof went up from the sides in the shape of a pyramid. Since our cots were placed along the sides, to sit on a cot, a man had to sit stooped over. It was only near the center of the tent that a man could stand upright. At the center was our stove, which was made from the top third of a gas drum with sand placed at the bottom of the firebox. Outside the tent was a gas drum filled with 100 octane gas from which a ¼" tubing brought the fuel to the stove. There was a ¼" valve at the stove to adjust the gas flow. All the parts of the stove came from wrecked B-24s.

Eventually, the Commanding Officer (CO) of the squadron decided that the gasoline was too expensive and dangerous. The squadron quartermaster personnel started delivering diesel oil. This went well until the metal smoke stacks became clogged with soot. Officers and enlisted men alike practiced a simple solution. Everybody but one man left the tent. He poured 100-octane gasoline into the stove and before running at full speed toward the door, threw a match into the gasoline soaked stove. The resulting blast shook the tent and blew the soot up and out of the chimney. Unfortunately the red-hot cinders that blasted out of the pipe landed on the nearest tents and often burned them to the ground. We called this a game of "blast your stove and burn a tent." I don't know how many tents were burned, but the guys that were burned out were the lucky ones since they were issued new tents and gear. The losers were the guys whose tents ended up only with holes in the roofs. As a consequence of this chimney cleaning operation, when the rains came (and there was a lot of that) it was nearly impossible to find a place in your tent that wasn't dripping wet.

Life on the ground between missions had its moments to remember. Take rodents, for example. Shooting rats or mice was entertainment. We all had survival kits with shotgun shells that fit into a .45 semi-automatic pistol. I guess the idea was that if you were shot down, you could always shoot a gourmet duck and eat it raw. I never knew of anyone that took one of those kits on a combat flight. We all carried our own 45's though. I took mine, threw a clip into it, put it in the pant leg pocket of my flying suit, and never took it out. I figured that if I was shot down and didn't win the war with eight shots, I would surrender. Fact is, the gun was so dirty it probably would have blown up in my hand—but back to the rats and mice. We set up a runway between a footlocker and the side of the tent. The hunter would sit very still until he heard something on the runway and then he would shoot into the runway getting himself a rat or a mouse. But he also got himself holes in the side of the tent. The sides on many tents had holes in them from the 'bee-bees' shots. You could hear these shots night or day, but no one panicked. It got so bad that the CO put out a camp stop order against shooting guns.

We learned not to take water for granted because every drop had to be delivered by truck and poured into a complex of 'Jerry' cans. We washed and shaved out of our helmets. As for the extake half of the equation, we distributed perforated one gallon cans buried to their hilt in the ground. No one had to walk more than a hundred feet to urinate. Had the war lasted much longer, I'm sure we would have reduced that to 20 feet. What amazed me was that no one ever stepped in one of those holes and broke an ankle.

Our outhouse was made of three 55-gallon drums that had been cut in half that rested on the ground with wooden seats. You had to climb several steps to get to them. The sides and the roof of the outhouse were built of wood giving a man a certain amount of privacy; and about four feet up the sides fine mesh screen was used to keep the flies out and to provide for ventilation. Usually, you met some one there and had an interesting chat or a chance to gossip and make a friend or an acquaintance. Ordinarily if you passed the man on the street pathways, you wouldn't have said hello to him. Additionally in the rainy season, it would pour down rain accompanied by wind. So when using the outhouse, a man could get a full shower while moving his bowels.

Life for the combat airmen was really very dull—that is, when we weren't flying and getting shot at. Other than guard duty, we were assigned few chores. If we weren't on a combat or training mission, we had the day to ourselves, so we read, slept, and sat around the officers' and enlisted men's clubs. But the real treat was a shower. The showers were available to all personnel at any time of the day or night, provided they were willing to make the mile-and-a-half trek down the road to the 376th Group Headquarters. Usually a group of men took off walking and, if luck were with them, they'd catch a ride. Guess this might be considered the war's equivalent of a pajama party! After a combat mission, dinner, and the mission critique, I would saunter over to the showers and sit there taking hot and cold showers. This routine became my own time for a personal critique of the mission. I would go through the mission over and over critiquing myself and evaluating what I had done right and what I had done wrong.

We had the time to see the towns in the area including San Pangrazio, which will never be on a tourist's "must see" list. At other times, we visited the larger towns that flanked San Pangrazio such as Lecci and Manduria; or we'd see Bari, one hundred miles to the north near the 'spur' of the Italian boot. We made it to Taranto, which was due west of our base and located on the inside of the heel of Italy. It was the site of the large Italian naval base that was occupied by the Allies.

7

Routine and Some Non-Routine Practices: November 1944

Protective Clothing and Gun Turret Operations
By Emmett (Mac) MacKenzie

To prepare one's self for physical protection during a sortie or a mission, we religiously followed a ritual. When the crew knew that a mission was coming up the next day, most crew members would take a shower and lay out clean long johns, two pairs of socks, G.I. boots, olive green wool or tan gabardine uniforms depending on the season, a sweater, a nylon flight suit that included a leather and fleece flight jacket and pants, and a fleece-lined billed cap. In the winter we'd just grabbed about every thing we could get our hands on.

At 5 a.m. the squadron's non-commissioned officer (NCO) shouted the wake-up call outside the doorway of the tent of each crew flying that day. It was a struggle to put on the layers of clothing in the dim light of the lantern. After breakfast, which was restricted to one half hour, all crews assigned to fly went to the flight equipment building located next door to the mess hall tent to pick up a parachute and a five-piece flying suit. Ten flak helmets and metal flak vests were always kept in the plane. Thankfully, this practice did not pertain to the parachutes, which were routinely removed from the plane by crewmembers after each flight and taken to the equipment building. In the same building the chutes were inspected, and stored for use by other crews. The inspection included checks for torn covers and nylon chute tears as well as for correct packing by the responsible chute packers. This was done once a week. Because of the appearance of many of the parachutes covers, one occasionally wondered if they had ever been inspected since the day that they left the factory. All one could do was to hope and pray that if the chutes were needed during a bailout, they would open correctly and save our lives.

Immediately after picking out their equipment, all the crews headed toward the trucks that lined up in front of the mess hall to take them to the planes on the flight line. Since no crew had its own plane, we were taken to the plane assigned to us at the Squadron Operations Center. It wasn't until our plane had taken off, rallied with other planes of our squadron, rendezvoused with the other squadrons of the 376th Group, and had reached an elevation of 10,000 feet the at Roy would tell us to move to our combat stations. Prior to this time, the only crewmen on station were the pilot, copilot, navigator, flight engineer, and the radio operator. The other crew members were lounging in the waist of the ship, except for Guy, or bombardier, who lounged in the nose of the plane and appeared to be sleeping soundly until the plane was within 30 minutes of the initial heading point (IP) of the ground target. When the call came for all of the crew to get ready for combat, each man removed his flight jacket and put on his heated outfit and all the other paraphernalia. The fleece-lined jacket and boots were plugged into the pants, which were then plugged into an outlet near each man's station. We all wore a fleece-lined flyer's skullcap too. It didn't take much imagination to realize the confinement imposed on our freedom of action while wearing a flak vest and a metal helmet over his other clothes during a bomb run. There was little room for any crewmember to perform his job comfortably.

Not surprisingly, no one could wear a chute pack because there simply was no room in the turrets. Normally, we placed the chutes either on the deck outside of the turrets, on the flight deck, or in the nose area of the plane. I was glad that we never had to bail out because once the plane was hit and disabled, the chutes would have bounced off the floor and sides of the ship making them difficult if not impossible to find in an emergency.

To keep warm, each crewman turned up the thermostat regulator on his suit as the temperature dropped to 50 or 60 degrees below zero as we climbed from 10,000 up to a maximum of 27,000 feet. In retrospect, these suits did a remarkably good job of keeping us warm.

Only after we returned from a mission and dropped down to about 10,000 or 12,000 feet did crew members begin to peel off the layers of their clothing until they were down to their dress uniforms and flight suits. At this point, the turret gunners would return to the waist section of the plane.

While talking to Roy in our motel room during the 50th Reunion of the 376th Bomb Group, I had the most unexpected and vivid flashback relating to one of our training missions while stationed at Charleston Airbase, South Carolina. We practiced dropping 100-pound dummy bombs on a huge target on the ground. Concentric painted circles radiated out from the big bull's eye at appropriate intervals from the center of the target. It was Guy's job to hit the bull's eye. A part of the training was devoted to developing a smooth technique for handing off the control of the plane from the pilot to the bombardier, who manned the

Norden Bomb Site. It was during this flashback that I remembered Guy had a problem lining up the plane with the target. The bomb (a flour sack filled with sand) was dropped with disastrous results. It landed outside the outer ring of the target in a cloud of dust. In retrospect, we thought it was quite funny but Roy didn't. He insisted on perfection with 100% target-hit accuracy.

Over and over again, Roy aligned the plane's course with the target (the Initial Point), set the plane on autopilot, and released control of the plane to Guy. Guy now had to make the final minute adjustments using the Norden Bomb Site and then drop the bomb. They repeated the procedure over and over until Guy made accurate drops one after the other.

Practice paid off handsomely when Guy, the lead bombardier on one mission of the 514th Squadron, was called on to obliterate the Hermann Goering Ball Bearing Plant in Vienna, Austria. It took Guy two runs before he successfully hit the target. It was bad enough to fly over Vienna once, but having to fly over it twice was crazy, but there was no other option. On this second bomb run, Guy had made a 100% hit on the target. It was to our joy and relief that he had done what was expected of him. Hurray for Guy!

The waist guns were manually operated and directly under the control of the gunners at all times. But the various turrets were operated with hand controls mounted on the turret itself and in front of the seated gunner. Each turret position had its built-in restrictions as to the "firing zone" available to it. The top turret (Martin), nose turret (Emerson), tail, top, and belly turret positions (Sperry) had special gun sights called "manually operated radian gun sights." Each turret was equipped with twin 50 caliber machine guns mounted on a plate as an integral part of the turret. Therefore, only the movement of turret, side to side or up and down, could direct the guns toward the enemy target plane. These movements were controlled by two hand controls mounted on the same table platform and were hydraulically operated by the gunner. The gun sight was located between the two guns.

My gunnery school instructor used an interesting analogy to help us learn to aim these huge guns and lead our targets. He told us to recall our days as paperboys when we learned to ride down the sidewalk and simultaneously roll and throw the newspaper ahead of the house so that it would land on the front porch. Of course, the analogy only went so far because the houses we hit with newspapers weren't flying at us at hundreds of miles an hour while trying to kill us with their machine guns.

The design of the one-piece radian gun sight was in the form of three concentric circles. The spokes were separated by the one-piece, cast-metal circles that emanated outward from the center. The distance between each of the three circles constituted a radian. These site radians were used to determine the lead the gunner had to allow for when aiming at the enemy plane. The lead on a target ranged from zero to three radians. One radian lead was used for a thousand yards, a two-radian lead was for two thousand yards, and a three-radian lead was for three thousand yards. The latter was the maximum lead possible with any degree of firing accuracy.

The concept of directing gunfire on a target was based on the premise that the bomber was at the center of a huge clock and that the target was located at the extremity of a very long hour hand. Twelve o'clock was beyond and in front of the nose of the plane, six o'clock was to the aft of the plane, three o'clock was off to the starboard side, and nine o'clock was off to the port side of the plane. The other eight points of the clock divided up those four points further just like the twelve numbers on the face of the clock. These reference numbers served to locate the enemy plane and to keep all the gunners informed as to the location of the incoming enemy plane.

Each gunner had a different firing zone, which was determined by the position of his gun. If the nose gunner was aiming at 12 o'clock and the tail gunner at 6 o'clock in line with the fuselage, their guns were pointing straight ahead and directly to the rear of the plane in line respectively with the longitudinal axis of the B-24. The radian measure would be zero. If the nose gunner aimed at 10 o'clock or 2 o'clock, he would give the target a two-radian lead, while the tail gunner would be aiming at 8 or 4 o'clock for the same radian lead. If either the tail or nose gunner were operating their guns at either outer edge of the firing zone, at 3 or 9 o'clock, their lead would be three radians. At these limits, the automatic stops would kick in and stop the guns from firing. A one-radian lead would be 5 and 6 o'clock for the tail gunner and 11 or 1 o'clock for the nose gunner.

A simple way of picturing the firing zone is to graphically visualize the gunner sitting at the center of a sphere within an equatorial plane representing the gun platform with zero degrees always aligned with the longitudinal axis of the aircraft. Then the region bounded by the longitudinal lines of +90 through -90 degrees and latitudinal lines of +45 through -45 degrees would determine the surface area of the sphere whose radius was a maximum of three thousand yards. Thus, the sculpted volume was the spatial region available to the gunner for firing his guns.

In the case of the belly turret, the zone of fire may be characterized as a hemispherical zone of fire. The gunner's position was the center of hemisphere that opened downward and whose edge was a great circle with a three-thousand-yard radius. The gunner could operate his turret and fire at any point within a hemispherical zone. Let's assume the gunner spotted an enemy plane off to the left of his turret at zero degrees and it was going to pass under his plane and head upward toward zero degrees in the same direction on the right side of the plane. If the turret operator's guns were at zero degrees, or horizontally inline with the enemy plane, he would have had to swing his guns downward through 90 degrees to reverse his direction through 180 degrees and then swing his guns upward from 90 through zero degrees to keep his target in site and in range. His effective operating range was +/-360 degrees. The turret's declination was limited to 90 degrees below a theoretical horizontal plane that contained the circle. Thus, the gunner could quickly vary his radian lead anywhere from zero to three radians or three to zero.

Similar to the belly turret, the top turret operated in a hemisphere that opened upward. The gunner's only handicap was the twin tail rudders that extended above the body of the B-24. Engineered into the operation of the turret were stops that prevented the 50 caliber guns from trimming off the rudders. Jim Snell was our top turret gunner, Andy Duval was our belly turret gunner, Byron Hunsicker was our tail turret gunner and I manned the nose turret guns.

The talent of the waist gunner, Lou Birnbaum, was severely restricted in the horizontal plane. If the target approached us at zero degrees elevation with respect to our plane and from either side, Lou had to be careful not to fire into either the tail rudders or the trailing edge of either wing. However each waist window position had its own moving zone of fire. The waist guns were operated manually and hence there were no turret stops on which to depend (a bird without tail or wing feathers has a severe handicap). Otherwise, all other elevations or declinations for firing within the firing zone were fair game.

The above scenarios are basic and only a few of the many possible combinations available to our gunners. It was the job of the gunner to be able to adapt his skills to any possible situation in which he found himself. With a radian site, rudimentary as it was, the task of aiming any one of the turrets at an enemy plane was relatively easy regardless of which direction it was approaching. With all this firepower, the B-24 was theoretically protected from all approaching enemy planes.

The Guessing Game
By Mike Ozkcus

Customarily, the next day's mission was posted inside squadron headquarters at about eight o'clock in the evening. The flying crews made it a point to check the list. If the pilot's name was on the list and scheduled to fly, then the crew was to fly also. If you were partying in one of the towns and didn't know if you were flying, then you phoned the squadron and asked, "Did Lt. Hatem make the team?" If yes, then you got back to the base as soon as you could; if no, then you continued partying.

One time I called from Bari and the answer was "Yes, Lt. Hatem has made the team." I had to get back but I forget who was with me. The evening mail truck heading south had already left. We drifted around town hoping, asking, looking, and praying for a ride. The prayers worked because right there in front of some sort of an official looking building was an unattended jeep. We popped right in and drove off heading south. Several hours later, we pulled up in front of squadron headquarters, left the jeep, and went back to our tents to get some sleep before the 5 o'clock wake-up call. The jeep remained in front of headquarters several days and then disappeared. I assume motor pool personnel took it and did whatever it took to make it ours.

In a related incident while flying for the Army Transport Command (ATC), I did the same thing in Labrador; but this time I had to sign the 104th Article of War and was fined seventy-five dollars, about one-half months pay. Now this is the first time that I have ever gone public with this confession, but now I know I'll be able to sleep better.

The Buzzing Craze

Buzzing an airfield was supposed to be done by crews that had finished their tour of duty and were on their way home. I do not remember any crew finishing its tour. But long before we thought of going home, Roy Hatem's crew buzzed inviting targets. Anyone who is familiar with the B-24 knows it defied all the principles of flying. Its designers took a railroad boxcar and put ample wings and enough horsepower on it to make it a great airplane. How any pilot could land that plane or buzz with it is beyond belief. Sitting in the pilot seats on the flight deck, it was nearly impossible to see the ground. Roy Hatem and Bill Anclam were great pilots and they proved it over and over again. One day the CO's wife had given birth to a boy. On returning from a mission, in a formation of six planes with Hatem leading, we buzzed the area. When we landed, we found out that we had flown so low that the bottoms of our planes were green from the olive trees we brushed.

Another time after a training flight, we buzzed the field over and over again. When we landed we were brought right to squadron headquarters and the CO stood there with a four-inch chimneystack that we had knocked down. That means we had to be at a maximum of twelve feet off the ground, but probably less.

Still contagious with the bug, we buzzed an Australian troop ship in the Tyrrhenian Sea located between Sardinia, the mainland Naples, and Sicily. All the Aussies ran to that side of the ship to see us. We were so low that they actually were looking and waving down at us and we waved and looked up at them. When we climbed and then dove down for another run on the other side of the ship, all the Aussies ran to the other side. It's a wonder that they didn't swamp the ship. I must point out that judging height over water is almost impossible, but Roy and Bill did it. They gave those Aussies something to remember. I know I do!

We continued to buzz everything in sight. One time we buzzed a flock of sheep and scattered them. Then we came back to buzz the shepherd. He stood there waving his hands, defying and cursing us. We knew that we were a bunch of bastards! We were getting our fun out of his pain because he had to round up those scattered sheep. When we landed, nobody mentioned the buzzing, but we never buzzed a living thing again. That didn't stop our buzzing though, and the CO never put out an order to stop it.

Bits and Pieces

At one point in our tour, we started flying crews to Naples for their rest leave at Capri. Paul O'Steen felt that we got these assignments because the CO thought we were getting "flakky." What he meant was that our crew and plane had been shot at by too many anti-aircraft guns. This meant more work for the "ground-grippers" i.e. the aircraft-mechanics.

Since Mac sat in the nose turret on these trips, he probably got the most of it, psychologically speaking, because of his position out in front and the fact that the turret was clear Plexiglas. My position was right behind him with small round Plexiglas windows on each side of the plane. The nose also had a floor that was mostly Plexiglas. It was mind-blowing to see everything rush past you at over 200 mph—especially the flak shells exploding all around like black popcorn. I don't know why we did these things, but we were young! We were going to live forever! We were the "chosen ones" and we were flying the "big ones."

I flew on Thanksgiving Day but I don't remember where. We were going to have a big turkey dinner that evening. When I got back to my tent, I cleaned up and put on a set of Class A dress military uniform and went to the club for a turkey dinner. It was a buffet style dinner. Everyone was seated, laughing, and were enjoying themselves, but there was not really anything worthwhile left of the turkey. So I put some of those table scraps on my plate and went over to the table where my friend, Chuck Parigian, had saved a seat for me. I sat down with my plate of scraps ready to speak to Chuck but he interrupted me by saying, "Mike, I don't feel well. I think I'm going to throw up. I have to leave" He got up and left without saying another word. I took his plate of drumsticks, white meat with all the trimmings and had a great Thanksgiving Dinner. The next day, Chuck was fine and so was I.

Crew 313 participated in the following missions 376th Group Mission No 358, November 6, 1944

Mission status:

- Target: Sarajevo, Yugoslavia; Ali Pasin Marshalling Yard
- Crew points: 1 sortie, 1 mission
- Total fight time: 4:45 hours
- Target distance: Approx. 220 miles (366 km)

Flight leaders:

- A Flight: Lt. Krines (513th Squadron)
- B Flight: Lt. Harris (512th Squadron)

Aircraft statistics:

- Aircraft at take off: 12
- Aircraft over target: 12
- Aircraft returning to base: 12
- Aircraft diverted or forced landing: 0

Total bomb load: 90 500-lb. bombs

Bombing results: None, formation did not drop bombs due to under cast. Orders were for visual only.

Fighter escort: None

Anti-aircraft: Heavy to scant and inaccurate.

Mission commentary: This was the first sortie flown by our 10-man crew. Our plane carried four 500-pound bombs. The record indicates that we did not fly with the 514th Squadron but filled out a box formation (usually four planes per box) with either the 512th or 513th Squadron that flew that day.

Path Finder Fix: Not used extensively before February 1945. But after that date, it became widely used, meaning that every squadron had at least one Path Finder Fix. The radar could see through clouds and under cast. It was located in what was formerly the location of the Sperry Ball Turret. A trained Radar Navigational Operator dropped bombs from the lead ship of the flight and the other planes in the box would follow suit.

376th Bomb Group Mission No. 361, November 8, 1944

Mission status:

- Target: Sjenica, Yugoslavia; troop concentration
- Crew points: 1 sortie, 1 mission
- Total flight time: 4:00 hours
- Target distance: Approx. 220 miles (366 km)

Flight leaders:

- A Flight: Col. Graff and Lt. Brown (515th Squadron)
- B Flight: Capt. Holsclaw (512th Squadron)

Aircraft statistics:

- Aircraft at takeoff: 14
- Aircraft over target: 14
- Aircraft returning to base: 12
- Aircraft diverted or forced landing: 0

Mission summary:

- Bomb load: 112 500-lb bombs
- Anti-aircraft: Heavy to scant and inaccurate
- Fighter escort: None
- Bombing results: No Path Finder Fix radar. Did not drop bombs due to weather.

- Mission commentary: Our plane carried eight 500-lb bombs. The anti-aircraft fire was heavy, scant, and inaccurate. The record indicates we did not fly with the 514th but filled out a box formation with either the 512th or 513th Squadron that flew that day. No other information available. Andy's comment: "Why did we have to bomb these German Troops? It isn't right." Did not drop bombs because of weather.

376th Bomb Group Mission No. 369, November 17, 1944

Mission status:

- Target: Vienna, Austria; Florisdorf Oil Refinery
- Crew points: 2 sorties, 1 mission
- Total flight time: 7:45 hours
- Target distance: Approx. 482 miles (801 km)

Flight leaders:

- A Flight: Maj. Snyder, Lt. Thomas (512th Squadron)
- B Flight: Lt. Nelson (514th Squadron)

Flight box configuration:

Lt. Thomas		A		
Lt. Brown	B		C	Lt. Nelson
Lt. Roeca		D		

Aircraft statistics:

- Aircraft at takeoff: 28

- Aircraft over target: 28

- Aircraft returning to base: 28

- Aircraft diverted or forced landing: 0

Mission summary:

- Bomb load: 265 500-lb bombs

- Bomb results: Path Finder Fix. No results photographed due to weather. Excellent run and brief glance at target indicated hits on north part of city.

- Fighter escort: 50 P-38s

- Anti-aircraft: Heavy to moderate and inaccurate

- Mission commentary: For another first, our crew flew with our own squadron carrying eight 500-lb bombs.

> **Paul's diary:** We raided the marshaling yards of Vienna today. Dropped 500-pound bombs through under-cast. On the way up we lost our own formation in the clouds, we flew the mission with another group. We saw lots of flak, but we used evasive action and avoided it. This was my first mission. Credit—two sorties or 1 mission.

> **Author's comment:** Paul was on sick leave for missions 358 and 361.

376th Bomb Group Mission 372, November 20, 1944

Mission status:

- Target: Zenica, Yugoslavia; railroad bridge
- Crew points: 1 sortie, 1 mission
- Total flight time: 5:20 hours
- Distance to target: 260 miles (494km)

Flight leaders:

- A Flight: Maj. Wimberley, Lt. Brown (515th Squadron)
- B Flight: Capt. Mackie (513th Squadron)

Aircraft statistics:

- Aircraft at takeoff: 28
- Aircraft over target: 27
- Aircraft returned to base: 28
- Aircraft diverted or forced landing: 0

Mission summary:

- Bomb load: 80 500-lb bombs
- Bomb results: No entry
- Anti-aircraft: None reported
- Fighter escort: None

- Mission commentary: Once again we flew with either the 513th or 515th Squadron, filling out a box formation. We were unable to locate primary target. One possible hit on alternate target, Fojnica Road bridge and secondary roads.

> **Paul's diary:** We went after a railroad bridge in Yugoslavia today with a bomb load of six 1,000-pound bombs. We did not bomb, as target was not visible. We defused the bombs and dropped the fuses in the Adriatic Ocean.

8

Varied Missions: December 2–15, 1944

By Emmett (Mac) MacKenzie

There was a difference in the British and American bombing strategies. The British Air Force bombed during the night. They first sent flights of spotter planes to drop incendiary bombs on the target and light it up. When the bombing crews came, they dropped their loads wherever fires were burning. The American Army Air Force bombed during the day. It claims that it had never been turned back from a target due to enemy action. This is true. Regardless of losses en route or at the target, the formation never turned back until after hitting the target or making a run on it.

There were just two air forces in Europe, the British 8th Air Force and the US 15th Air Force. (The Halverson Group of B-24s was sent to Africa to stop Rommel's thrust into Egypt in 1942. The group was designated the 9th Air Force then, but in 1943, its name was changed to the 15th Air Force.) In a little over three years of its existence, the British 8th Air Force, stationed in England, lost over forty thousand men. While I was in Italy, a *Stars and Stripes* newspaper article said that in the same year, the US 15th Air Force lost fifty percent of its personnel and one hundred percent of its planes, about seven hundred and fifty planes.

There had been times when whole squadrons did not return to base. Using the advanced Norden Bomb Sight, they bombed their targets with a degree of precision previously unknown. This was known as "strategic bombing," which has the goal of destroying the enemy's capacity to produce and distribute war material. We never flew missions in Europe for the purpose of bombing regions, only specific military targets. I do not recall ever bombing where the target was not visible. If there was an under-cast at the target, we usually went to a secondary target. When radar became available, we could bomb through the clouds.

The British 8th Air Force lost eighty planes and about a thousand men when it hit the Schwenfurt ball bearing plant. However, the temporary slow down in bearing production did trickle on down to all phases of German industry and retarded its efforts. Vehicles without bearings don't move! I am sure that if our intelligence suspected that a horse somewhere in Germany or Austria being groomed to pull a wagon of contraband, we would have precision bombed it to bits and pieces.

Night Mission: One Plane, One Crew

Three crews had volunteered to fly separate night harassment missions. Each plane and its crew had its own target as determined by our squadron headquarters. Coincidentally, it was three years to the day, that the Japanese had bombed Pearl Harbor, and Roy had volunteered our crew to fly this night mission alone. Roy wanted to rack up some more rotation points for himself and his crew. We received rotation points when we completed missions and sorties. We needed 50 points to be able to go home.

The mission scenario went as follows: Having obtained a list of crews from the 514th Headquarters that were to fly on a particular day, the on-duty NCO jeep driver screeched to a stop in front of each crew's tent and woke them up. The driver pounded on our tent door and yelled at us to roll out of our sacks and to get going. It was 1:00 in the morning. Someone of our crew lit the lantern. We dressed in the cold tent, locked the tent door as we left, and headed to the mess hall, which was always open for such occasions.

Next, we headed to the parachute tent, some fifty feet away to pick up our chutes, flying suits, and other gear. The cold and dry night air hit us in the face as we threw our gear into the waiting jeep that would take us out to the assigned plane's parking ramp. The enlisted men "walked the props through." Each man took a single propeller blade and walked it through about a 120-degree arc to lubricate the engine. Then Paul started the small Jenny Starter Engine unit. This was a two-horsepower gas engine, like a lawnmower engine, located near the bomb bay. It provided enough electricity to power the starter motors for each engine. After all of the plane's engines and systems checks had been made, we climbed aboard and took our place in the waist of the plane. Each of us had time to pause and take stock of what the future would be. Would this be our last time to take off from the runway? Roy set the brakes, revved up the engines, and tested them to determine if they were all functioning properly. Convinced that they were OK, he released the brakes and taxied the plane from the parking pad to the bumpy meshed metal strips that comprised the runway. Having made a 180-degree turn at the end of the runway, Roy jammed the four engine throttles forward and the plane took on a life of its own, picking up speed until the sound of the tires on the steel planks faded way. We were now airborne. The air became even more cold and crisp as we climbed into the black night sky filled with stars shining brightly down on us. While each gunner hunkered down in his own fleece lined flying suit while contemplating the future, the four busiest crew members—Roy, the pilot, Bill, the copilot, Paul, the flight engineer, and Mike, our navigator—were spared the opportunity to ponder the imponderables.

The Beginning of the Roughest Month

It was December 7, 1944, and our crew was scheduled for a mission to Lenz, Austria, nearly seven hundred miles from San Pangrazio. We went through the usual routine of flight readiness checks before taking off. As our plane lumbered out onto the runway in preparation for take off, nothing seemed to be particularly different from the other missions our crew had flown.

North of the base, our squadron rendezvoused with the other three squadrons and set out for the target, first flying over the Adriatic Sea, and then heading for the Yugoslavian Alps. Normally, the Alps glistened in the brilliant light of the morning sun and especially the isolated and highest peak. It was monolithic, conical, and prism-like, and served as a landmark for us in clear weather. Its slab-like reddish granite sides thrust up and beyond the surrounding mountain peaks and assured us that we were on the correct heading.

But the closer we flew toward the Alps, the thicker, wetter, and darker the clouds became until we were flying in a sea of gray soup with no visual reference point. The weather became so bad that the group commander told the squadron commanders to break off the mission and head back to the base. By this time, we could no longer see the squadron formation or the planes in our own flight box formation. Roy, following instructions, broke off and thought it would be best to climb above the storm and head for clear skies. Then Mike could get his bearings and plot a course back to the base. However, as our B-24 struggled to gain altitude, the wings began to ice up rapidly and the four Pratt & Whitney R-1830 engines labored painfully to pull the plane forward and upward. At some point during this Herculean effort, the plane began to "mush around" as the air became more and more unstable and incapable of supporting the plane's weight. The engines could no longer pull the plane upward and the wings began to lose their lifting power.

The plane had risen over 20,000 feet by this time. It became apparent to both Roy and Bill that our plane was struggling against the odds of breaking through the sea of dense, roiling, gray clouds. If we couldn't break through the clouds, we could stall out and possible go into a flat spin from which we couldn't recover. There was no time left to adequately prepare the crew for what Roy was about to do next, except to bark out over the intercom, "Grab something and hold on tight, we're going down!" To avoid stalling out, he pushed the nose of the plane over and it plunged down rapidly, plowing down further and further into an unknown morass. The idea behind this maneuver was to drop down far enough so the ice would break off the wings, having picked up greater speed and then swing the plane upward and accelerate to maximum speed to break out of the storm clouds. The only question in each man's mind was whether our plane and crew could make it safely through this maneuver. No one would know for the next few minutes.

The turret gunners were seated and relatively safe, but it was Mike, Guy, Paul, and Lou who had to make sure they were hanging on to something substantial. If the crewman was standing on the flight deck, seated at the radio operator's desk, or located in the nose of the plane, as were the navigator and bombardier, there were only seconds left to heed Roy's warning to avoid being tossed helter-skelter around the plane's interior. With the greatest of effort, these crewmen struggled to make their torsos and legs obey their minds, for each body extremity would attempt to go in its own chosen direction. Adding to the dilemma, anything that was not tied down would be flying around as if it had a life of its own, refusing to obey the law of gravity.

I was in the nose turret and felt like I was frozen in a slowly moving time frame. As our plane dove, every second seemed to take on a dimension of timelessness. The downward force of the plane seemed to press in and about me on all sides. At one point, I remembered looking out of the left side of my turret's clear plastic dome and wonder why the wing seemed to be standing on end above my turret. A case of vertigo. There was nothing for the other crewmembers to do but to trust that Roy and Bill would use everything they knew to get them out of this precarious situation.

After the plane had dropped about twenty thousand feet, Roy swung the nose upward in a second attempt to climb above the storm. He pushed the engine throttles all the way forward, but to no avail. The other crewmembers could do nothing except to ride out each attempt while watching globs of gray mist race quickly by as we descended once again for another try. The maneuver to break free was attempted a third time. To rise above the storm, Roy nosed the plane upward once again and applied all his skills to increase the speed of the plane to its maximum. Struggling with all their might, our pilots had finally succeeded in breaking through the morass of clouds into that allusive sunlit sky about us.

Roy was now able to level off the plane so that Mike could do his job of establishing a reference point from which to set a course to get the plane and crew back to the base. But the greatest sight for all of us was to see that glorious sunlight bouncing off huge billowy, white cumulous clouds around and below our plane. The crew could finally relax and realize that they were going to make it back to San Pangrazio. Having descended below twelve-thousand feet and headed out over the Adriatic toward the base, the gunners and Guy took up their normal noncombatant positions in the plane and shed their helmets, flack vests, and heated suits.

The effort and energy expended to save the crew and plane only became indelibly apparent after we had landed, and the plane was sitting on parking pad. It was as if Roy and Bill had just emerged from a heavy rain shower. Their uniforms were dripping wet with perspiration while the strain of their efforts showed through the sweat on their faces.

Paul and Jim also had problems, which gave rise to much stress, exhaustion, and sweat-soaked uniforms. On at least one occasion after dropping our bomb and heading back to base, our plane was hit by flak causing serious damage to the electrical and hydraulic systems. In this instance, the problems were the result of as many as 125 flak holes penetrating the plane. Paul and Jim attempted to fix or jerry-rig the failing or damaged equipment.

That day was just one of those special days that the crew owed their lives to Roy and Bill. Roy had kept his continuing promise to get the crew back home safely. We were never as glad as when we were able to jump out of the plane and plant our feet on the parking pad.

Crew 313 participated in the following missions 376th Bomb Group, Mission No. 376, December 2, 1944

Mission status:

- Target: Straszhof, Czechoslovakia; railroad marshalling yards and Florisdorf Refinery
- Alternate target: Sastin, Czechoslovakia
- Crew points: 2 sorties, 1 mission
- Total flight time: 6:40 hours
- Distance to target: 495 miles (803 km)

Flight leaders:

- A Flight: Major Taylor and Lt. Reno (514th Squadron)
- B Flight: Capt. Holsclaw (513th Squadron)

Aircraft statistics:

- Aircraft at takeoff: 34
- Aircraft over target: 29

- Aircraft returned to base: 33
- Aircraft lost: 0
- Aircraft damaged: 0

Flight box configuration:

Lt. Reno		A		
Lt. Albrecht	B		C	Lt. Ford
Lt. Clark		D	E	Lt. Miller

Mission summary:

- Bomb load: 226 500-lb bombs

- Anti-aircraft: Heavy, moderate, inaccurate

- Bomb results: Path Finder Fix radar. Due to cloud cover, hit alternate. Columns of smoke at 25,000 ft. indicate good results.

- Mission commentary: Losing #4 engine and feathering it was followed by almost loosing #3 engine, both on the same side of the plane. Fuel had to be transferred gradually to the right wing cells so that the wing tanks could be balanced with those of the left wing cells. The #3 and #4 props were feathered, and concurrently the flaps and ailerons were adjusted to ensure the stabilization and control of the plane.

> **Paul's diary:** "Our target today was the marshaling yards at Vienna. Twenty minutes from the target, we lost all the oil in F#4 engine and had to feather it. We were losing all the oil in #3 engine; and I thought we would lose that one also. We dropped out of the formation and turned back. We bombed a road in Austria."

> *Author's comment: Paul's entry does not match the account in The Liberandos by James Walker.*

514th Squadron (Night) Mission No. 379, December 7, 1944

Mission status:

- Target: Innsbruck, Austria
- Crew points: 2 sorties, 0 mission
- Flight time: 5:35 hours
- Distance to target: 523 miles (842 km)

Flight leaders:

- A Flight: Lt. Brainard (512th Squadron)
- B Flight: Roy Hatem (514th Squadron)
- C Flight: Lt. Dale (515th Squadron)

Aircraft statistics:

- Aircraft at takeoff: 3
- Aircraft over target: 0
- Aircraft returned to base: 3, 1due to engine failure
- Aircraft failed to attack due to cloud: 2

Mission summary:

- Bomb load: 24 500-lb bombs
- Bomb results: Bombs not dropped
- Path Finder Fix: None

> **Paul's diary:** This was a night mission. We took off at 2:00 a.m. Our target was Innsbruck, Austria. We were supposed to fly in cloud coverage all the way to avoid night fighters. Over the Alps the weather cleared and according to orders, we turned back. Bomb load was 8 500-lb. bombs. We dropped them in the Adriatic on the way back.

376th Bomb Group, Mission No. 383, December 15th 1944

Mission status:

- Target: Innsbruck, Austria; railroad marshalling yards
- Crew points: 2 sorties, 1 mission
- Flight time: 5:35 hours
- Target distance: Approx. 523 miles (869 km)

Flight leaders:

- A Flight: Capt. Kornrumph, Capt Ford (512th Squadron)
- B Flight: Capt. Ford (513th Squadron)
- C Flight: Lt. Kremer
- D Flight: Capt. Albrecht

Flight box configuration:

Capt. Ford	A		
Lt. Clark	B	C	Lt Kremer
Capt. Albrecht		D	

Aircraft statistics:

- Aircraft at takeoff: 28
- Aircraft over target: 27
- Aircraft returned to base: 25
- Aircraft diverted or forced landing: 2
- Aircraft lost: 1 due to anti-aircraft
- Aircraft damaged: 2 major, 1 minor

Mission summary:

- Bomb load: 259 500-lb bombs
- Bombing results: Superior. 76% of bombs hit squarely in railroad marshalling yards. Much of the rolling stock and tracks were destroyed. One box formation hit town of Schwas, Austria.
- Casualties/Missing: 11 missing, 1 lightly wounded
- Anti-aircraft: Heavy, intense, and accurate
- Fighter escort: 30 P-38s and 12 P-51s
- Mission commentary: No entry indicating that the 514th Squadron flew. Therefore our crew once again flew with either the 512th or 513th Squadrons. Our plane carried 8 500-lb bombs.

Paul's diary: Those peaks coming up though the clouds really looked rugged. Target was clear. They really shot hell out of us with that flak. Several bursts right outside the cockpit. Could see the red flames, they were so close. The lead ship went down somewhere in the Alps. Think the crew bailed out. Counted numerous holes in the ship after we landed. We certainly had our baptism of fire today, but none of the crew was injured. We knocked hell out of the railroad yards.

9

The Worst of Times: December 17–29, 1944

Deadly Targets
By Mike Ozckus

In terms of dangerous targets, I classified Vienna, Austria (the Big V as we called it) with its Floresdorf Oil Refinery as the most deadly due to both the huge number of flak guns (1,600) and the accuracy of their gunners. Next would come Lenz and Innsbruck, Austria, then two targets in Northern Italy, Verron (the Little V), and Brenner Pass. However, it only takes one gun to knock you down. If that gun is at that target when you are there, then the number of guns is not important.

I did not keep a record or a log of my sorties. While I can recall some of the times we came home crippled, I cannot put the blame on any one target for certain. In addition, about one third of my sorties were flown with other crews. It is difficult to separate events that occurred when I was with my crew and those that occurred while I was flying with other crews.

On one particular mission, we had our hydraulic brakes shot away. Roy Hatem brought us in with no brakes. We could not have had better pilots than Roy and Bill Anclam, but that goes for each man on that crew. Roy and Bill just skidded the plane to the side of the runway and off the landing strip. The crew suffered not one scratch. When the ambulance drove up, I asked the driver, "What the hell are you doing here? Get the hell out of here. We don't need you." He said that he was just doing his job. I apologized, and seeing that no one needed help, he drove off. I had lost my cool, something I never did. But it must have been one nerve wracking bitch of a mission to make me lose it. The next day, the 514th Bomb Squadron must have had a tough time fielding a team.

Innsbruck, Austria is a tourist city in the middle of the Alps. All it had was a railroad marshalling yard. It was located in a valley and surrounded by mountains on all sides. There was only one way in and one way out. The direction of our approach gave the ground anti-aircraft gunners at the target site our heading for the target. They probably had men at lookout sites on the mountaintops. They could have easily thrown rocks at us from these positions. With simple trigonometric calculations, they could determine' our height and relay the information to the anti-aircraft gunners. That's all they needed.

I believe that it was a training flight. I can remember the beatings we took but cannot pin them down or place them on any specific target. There were no foxholes in the skies. When we flew the bomb run, we took what they had to offer. That meant that we were under fire for six to twenty minutes. On one mission the meteorologist figured a tailwind and a six-minute run. The tailwind turned out to be a headwind and a twenty-minute run. I do not believe that there are many duck hunters today from that group that made those runs.

We hit Innsbruck, several times, but I believe this time it was just a squadron effort. In one of the planes in the flight, the pilot and copilot were brothers. The copilot had a crew of his own but since it was his first combat mission he flew with a crew that had combat experience, as was squadron policy. This crew included his brother. After hitting Innsbruck, we broke for home. Someone reported over the intercom that plane number so and so was falling behind. I looked through my astrodome and saw a stream of gas pouring out of their right wing. Nothing else seemed to be wrong, but the brothers and their plane could not keep up. Our crew kept an eye on them and when they lost them in the middle of the Alps, I noted the coordinates in my log. All this went to the de-briefing officer. Months later, the navigator returned to base. He was nothing but skin and bones. The following is his story.

The crew's plane cleared the Alps and got to northern Italy where the land was flat. The pilot gave the word to bailout. The last to leave the plane were the pilot and copilot, as was expected of them. Partisans rescued many of the crew but not the pilot and copilot. Hitler's national police, the Gestapo, got to them first in armored vehicles and the partisans felt the cost would have been too high to rescue them.

To be taken prisoners by the German military was the best of the possible situation. The military treated its captives with the respect due prisoners of war. We were told to surrender to them whenever possible.

Surrendering to civilians, civilian authorities, or the Gestapo was a different story. For example, the Croatians in Yugoslavia were Nazi allies. They hanged American airmen.

The Office of Strategic Services (O.S.S.), the equivalent of the military side of the C.I.A., and its British equivalent had set up camps in enemy-held Yugoslavia and northern Italy. The purpose of these camps was to transmit information to the allies and to provide for and stay in touch with the partisans. They also provided refuge for downed airmen. Their camps were about thirty miles apart.

Accompanied by the partisans, these airmen walked during the night only from camp to camp. All they had for food from the partisans was a handful of dried corn each day. It took several nights of walking to get from one camp to another. Traveling in this manner, it took them 108 days to reach an allied landing strip in Yugoslavia where a C-47 picked them up and flew them to Bari, Italy, the headquarters for the 15th Air Force. The navigator's biggest gripe was that the rescued crew members had to stand for hours in Bari on their bare feet on the cold tile before someone helped them. When I talked to him, he was literally skin and bones, but then he was on his way home.

A Christmas Present for Hall, Austria

I can remember the town of Hall, Austria. If you can locate it on a map, you might mistake it for a flyspeck. Probably its biggest crime was that it had two railroad tracks. No big thing happened there, it was a milk run, but I remember it only because we hit it on Christmas day.

Prelude to Mission 393
By Mike Ozkcus and Emmett (Mac) MacKenzie

On December 27, Paul O'Steen concluded his diary notes with a couple of simple statements: "We came back and landed O.K. I wonder how long our luck will hold out." The latter statement was to be prophetic. As anyone could see from our Sorties/Missions flight record, December was a busy month for our crew. We had flown eleven missions including two aborted missions. The first mission to be aborted was a harassment night mission over Lenz, Austria. It was only aborted after we ran out of cloud cover over the Yugoslavian Alps. The second aborted mission occurred when we encountered a critical fuel leak on take off from our base. Nevertheless, we were all getting tired and to say the least, we were all a little edgy.

The Brenner Pass connected Austria with northern Italy. It was through this pass that the German military supplied its troops. To halt this troop supply, we bombed the roads. The Germans would repair them, and we would bomb them again. The target of the December 29 mission was another bridge in the Brenner Pass area. The Germans were continuing in their attempt to escape from Italy by road and railway, taking with them their supply trucks, personnel carriers, and tanks as the Allied forces pushed them closer and closer to the Italian-Austrian boarder. The Germans had organized a heavy concentration of anti-aircraft guns in the pass area to challenge and prevent American air power from hindering their escape.

The stage was set for the engagement of firepower directed from both sides toward each other. The 15th Air Force ordered many elements of its 47th wing to fly. The wing was comprised of comprised of B-24 and B-25 bomber units along with fighter groups to engage the Germans in an all out effort over a week's period to prevent the Germans from escaping. The 376th HBG was to drop 145 1,000-pound bombs that day. It was our mission to blow up a bridge, and to disrupt and hinder the German's escape route into Austria.

Our plane, along with the other planes of the 514th Squadron, dropped bombs that day. The results were superior. Seventy-two percent of the bombs dropped on and around the bridge were within a 1,000-foot radius. Our crew and plane had been participating in one after another of these rough missions.

No one expected or could have anticipated the end of this very memorable event as it unfolded on that day for Andy Duval and the rest of crew No. 313. It was on this day that we suffered our first personnel casualty and earned our first purple heart. Andy, our Sperry Ball turret gunner, was hit in the foot. Normally during flight the turret is lowered to protect our underbelly from fighters but during the bomb run it is raised and vacated because the gunner couldn't get out of it in an emergency.

It was Lou Birmbaum, our radio operator, who told us over the intercom that Andy was hit. Lou was crying. The two were very close. The men in the waist of the plane made Andy comfortable until Guy Bretilotte, the bombardier and the first aid officer, could get back there and give him a shot of morphine which eased things for him.

Roy handled this situation very well. He asked me for a direct heading home and the altitude of the most favorable winds. I gave it to him and he immediately broke away from the formation, poured on the gas and got Andy back to the base. A red flare was shot on landing for a wounded man and the ambulance followed us until we stopped and unloaded Andy. We all worried about the wound, but in a week's time he was back in the U.S.A. and recovered very well.

Andy's Last Mission (as related by Roy)

As a standard procedure, Andy was not in his belly turret while over the target area. Instead, he was just standing in the waist area of the plane watching all the anti-aircraft shells explode around our plane. It was as if the flak was comprised of dozens of black popcorn balls that suddenly appeared out of nowhere to seek their intended victims. If you could see the black puffs of smoke, you knew you were probably safe because the shell had already exploded. In the event of any major damage to the plane or injury to its personnel occurred, an alert would have been sounded quickly. It's the shell explosion that you can't see that is dangerous to the ship and crew alike!

Suddenly, Andy felt a powerful, numbing, and painful blow to in his right foot. He knew he had been hit. As soon as the initial shock had passed, he got on the intercom and said he had been hit and needed help. Roy told Guy to get back to where Andy lay. When Guy arrived, Andy's boot was still on his foot and blood was oozing out of the hole in the toe of the boot. Guy grabbed a nearby parachute and made a pillow for Andy's head. Then Guy searched his medical kit for morphine and gave it to Andy. Then Guy tried to stop the bleeding with a tourniquet placed around the leg, all to no avail. In desperation, Guy called Roy and told him he was out of options. Roy turned control of the plane over to Bill and headed back to the waist of the plane. He quickly assessed the problem and removed Andy's boot so that the cold temperature would freeze the foot and stop the bleeding. It did. Turning to Guy, he told him to keep watch over Andy; then Roy headed back to the cockpit.

Normally, Roy would put the plane on autopilot and set it for 225 mph, then sit back and relax. But this day was different. Autopilot control wouldn't do. He revved the engines and soon was flying as fast as the plane could go. At 300 mph, it was the fastest flight that this particular plane was ever to make.

Meanwhile, Lou called the base at San Pangrazio and asked headquarters to clear the runway before our plane arrived and asked to have an ambulance standing by. It was a bright sun shiny day as we raced back to base. Every one was anxious to get Andy back so that he could receive proper medical treatment.

As the base came into sight, Roy lowered the flaps and zoomed-in for a quick landing. Our plane had been cleared for an immediate landing. He taxied the plane to a designated parking pad, cut the engines, and raced to open the bottom hatch in the waist of the plane so Andy could be removed. The ambulance and medics were standing by and shortly thereafter, the ambulance headed for the base hospital. Later when Andy's condition was stabilized, the doctors told Andy he was one of the lucky ones. His toes were all intact and he only had received a non-debilitating injury to the metatarsal bone. Members of the crew visited him until he was shipped home two weeks later on a transport ship. Andy's departure left an indelible mark on the crew's psyche. Not much was said, but those crewmembers that remained would always miss his presence. We were no longer a whole or a complete crew.

Ironically, on-board radar sights, the Pat Finder Fix radar, were just beginning to be installed on B-24 in the belly turret gunner's position.

As a postscript, Andy was hospitalized for several months and was one of the first GIs to receive the benefits of a government-sponsored educational program for all returning veterans. The program was to become known as the GI Educational Bill of Rights (or simply the GI Bill). It guaranteed an educational opportunity at whatever best fitted the needs and desires of the veterans. Andy attended college and received a degree in electrical engineering. Shortly thereafter, he married his childhood sweetheart, Jeannette, who was by then a Registered Nurse.

My Last Mission
By Andre Duval

December 29th was my last mission. I received a flak wound in my left foot. Just prior to the bomb run on this mission (Brenner, Italy, a railroad bridge), my judgment was that the automatic positioning control of the ball turret malfunctioned. I used the manual capability to orient the turret to enable the opening of the hatch, and climbed up into the plane as discussed on the intercom with Roy. I manned one of the waist-gun positions and alternated from one to the other on the early part of the bomb run. Lou had positioned himself in a prone position with his head peering into the open bomb bay watching the bombs drop away toward the target and a strike. Suddenly, my left foot rose up off the floor and felt as though a hammer had struck it from under the floor. As my intercom wires about my chest were severed, I had to manually arouse Lou and point for him to observe. Lou, Guy, and Roy attended to me. I do not recall details at this point. They laid me down and covered me, as I was very cold. The electrical heated suit I wore was destroyed. I believe Roy was the first of our squadron to land and an ambulance met us. From there, I was taken to an Army Air Force field hospital where x-rays were taken and a cast was put on my leg covering my toes up to a point above the knee. The injury was the first metatarsal bone in the left foot where about 1/2" of bone was gone. At this field hospital, orders were written for my evacuation to states-side for possible bone and tendon graft.

I wrote a letter home and I lied for the first time. I told my parents that I was not wounded badly and that I expected to return to duty. This letter got to my mother the day before an officer brought a brief telegram indicating I was seriously wounded in combat. Thoughtfully, Roy wrote a nice letter to my Mom and Dad.

From the field hospital, I was brought to an Army Air Force hospital in Bari, Italy then I was sent to an Army hospital just outside of Naples. I think the process took about two months. I was eventually evacuated by way of Naples on a Coast Guard troop carrier, the General Yates. I was brought on board as a litter patient and was assigned to the ship's sickbay. This was first class passage. Of special note, a school chum was a cook aboard the ship and he recognized me while I was lying on a litter on the dock prior to loading. He frequently visited me in the sick bay bringing such goodies as cake, coke, and ice cream. The ship entered New York harbor ten days later.

I was temporarily placed in a hospital in Hempstead, Long Island. While there, I was visited by Mrs. Hatem who, at the time, was very much with child. This is another evidence of Roy's professionalism and loyalty to the crew because he somehow followed my whereabouts and progress. It was here that I met Jeannette, whom I married in August 1947. My sister also visited me there.

Next was the hospital at Camp Divans, in Massachusetts. My itching and smelling cast was removed and by this time, the big toe of my left foot had moved backwards and closed the gap in the metatarsal and the bone graft. I was able to move the big toe, thus no tendon graft was in order. This was all good.

Soon, I was sent to a convalescence hospital at Plattsburg, Barracks in Plattsburg, New York where, on July 27, 1945, I received a medical discharge with a 50% disability. This was reduced to 20% disability a year later and is still retained.

Crew 313 participated in the following missions 376th Bomb Group Mission No. 385, December 17, 1944

Mission status:

- Target: Salzburg, Austria, railroad marshalling yards
- Crew points: 2 sorties and 1 mission
- Flight time: 7:20 hours
- Target distance: Approx. 570 miles

Flight leaders:

- A Flight: Capt. Turner, Lt. Bishop (515th Squadron)
- B Flight: Lt. Roeca (513th Squadron)

Flight box configuration:

Lt. Bishop	A		
Lt. Carlson	B	C	Lt Roeca
Lt. Henry	D		

Aircraft statistics:

- Aircraft at takeoff: 27
- Aircraft over target: 24
- Aircraft returned to base: 25
- Aircraft diverted or forced landing: 2
- Aircraft lost: 0

- Aircraft damaged: 2 major, 1 minor

Mission summary:

- Bomb load: 204 500-lb bombs

- Airmen casualties: 1 lightly wounded

- Bomb results: The bombing results were superior. Seventy five percent of the direct hits noted on rail yard and storage area. One box dropped on town of Villlach.

- Anti-aircraft: Heavy, moderate, and accurate

- Fighter escort: P-38s flew cover for the mission

- Mission commentary: Only the 513th and 515th Squadrons flew that day, therefore our crew and plane must have taken up a "filler" slot inasmuch as our squadron was not flying. Our plane was loaded with 8 500-lb bombs.

> **Paul's diary:** We are going after a railroad yard at Salzburg, Austria today. The Alps are becoming a familiar sight for me. Most of our missions are behind the Alps. The earth was hazy but the target was visible. Flak was pretty heavy. A piece came through the cockpit and passed between me and the pilot (I was standing directly behind him). It was so close, the broken glass from the window hit me on the hand. Don't know how it missed both of us, but it did, thank God. The missions are getting rough. Hope we hold out until we finish, and by the grace of God, we will.

376th Group Mission No. 388, December 21, 1944

Mission status:

- Target: Rosenheim, Germany; railroad marshalling yard

- Crew points: 0 sortie and 1 mission

- Flight time: 7:00 hours
- Target distance: Approx. 590 miles (951 km)

Flight leaders:

- A Flight: Maj. Korntumph, Lt. Hoover (513th Squadron)
- B Flight: Lt. Parvin (515th Squadron)

Flight box configuration:

Lt. Hoover		A		
Lt. Schusler	B		C	Lt. Parvin
Lt. Carlson		D		

Aircraft statistics:

- Aircraft at takeoff: 26
- Aircraft over target: 3
- Aircraft returned to base: 22
- Aircraft diverted or forced landing: 4
- Aircraft lost: 0
- Aircraft damaged: 0

Mission summary:

- Bomb load: 220 500-lb bombs
- Bomb results: Complete cloud cover. Path Finder Fix radar operator concluded target was well saturated.

- Anti-aircraft: No report was made as to the anti-aircraft firing accuracy

- Airmen casualties: None

- Fighter escort: 36 P-51s

- Mission commentary: Our squadron once again did not fly, however, our crew and plane filled in a box position with either the 513th or 515 Squadrons, which did fly that day.

> **Paul's diary:** We went to Rosenheim, Germany today. More railroad marshalling yards. They seem to be our priority targets. We bombed through an under-cast. Didn't see any flak this trip. This didn't make me mad at all. The weather was bad coming back. Cockpit iced up due to the intense cold at 27,000 feet, which was our altitude. We had to break formation to keep from colliding with our own ships.

376th Group Mission 389, December 25, 1944

Mission status:

- Target: Hall, Austria; main railroad marshalling yards

- Crew points: 2 sortie, 1 mission

- Flight time: 7:20 hours

- Target distance: Approx. 540 miles (898 km)

Flight leaders:

- A Flight: Maj. Taylor, Capt. Reno (514th Squadron)

- B Flight: Lt. Carlson (512th Squadron)

Flight box configuration:

Capt. Reno		A		
Capt. McChesney	B		C	Lt. Roeca
Lt. Schusler		D		

Aircraft statistics:

- Aircraft over target: 27
- Aircraft returned to base: 25
- Aircraft diverted or forced landing: 2
- Aircraft lost: 1

Mission summary:

- Bomb load: 191 500-lb bombs
- Bomb results: Failure
- Anti-aircraft: Heavy, moderate, and inaccurate
- Casualties: 10 men missing
- Mission commentary: Overshot the target by 1,500–6,000 ft. No fighter escort sighted. No report was made as to the anti-aircraft firing accuracy.

> **Paul's diary:** December 25, 1944. Today is Xmas and we went on another raid. Peace on earth, good will toward men. Seems out of place with me this year. We went to Hall, Austria. Still knocking out the German railroads. Saw plenty of snow this Xmas, but it was all on the Alps. They shot plenty of flak up at us, but we turned off just before we came in range of it. The weather was clear, and we could see the bombs on the target. Our formation

> lost another ship, this time due to engine trouble. Lost them right after the target. Don't know where they went, but hope they bailed out.
>
> December 26, 1944 (an extraneous entry). We are scheduled to fly again tomorrow. We think it will be Brenner Pass. Our squadron went up today and had hell blown out of them, but they didn't get the bridge they went after. This seems to be our worst target and everyone is sweating it out. A friend of mine caught a piece of flak in the head, but he is going to be O.K.

376th Bomb Group Mission, No. 391, December 27, 1944

Mission status:

- Target: Bressaone, Italy; railroad bridge
- Crew points: 0 sortie and 0 missions
- Flight time: 2:50 hours
- Target distance: Approx. 532 miles (898 km)

Flight leaders:

- A Flight: Col. Snyder, Capt Miller (512th Squadron)
- B Flight: Lt. Dale (515th Squadron)
- C Flight: Lt. Smith (513th Squadron)

Flight box configuration:

Col. Snyder, Capt. Miller		A		
Lt. Dale		B	C	Lt. Smith

Aircraft statistics:

- Aircraft at takeoff: 22

- Aircraft over Target: 19

- Aircraft returned to base: 22

- Aircraft lost: 0

Mission summary:

- Bomb load: 94 1,000-lb bombs

- Bomb results: Satisfactory. Only three direct hits on bridge.

- Anti-aircraft: Heavy to moderate and accurate.

- Mission commentary: Our crew and plane flew as a filler crew. The mission was lead by Col. Snyder and Capt. Miller of the 512th Squadron.

> **Paul's diary:** December 27, 1944: We started for Brenner Pass today. Immediately after take off, we developed a bad gas leak in the bomb bay. We circled the field waiting for instructions. They advised us to use up all the gas we could, and get rid of the five 1,000 pound bombs we were carrying. The ship was full of gas fumes and in extreme danger of exploding if the least spark was struck. I used the emergency release on the nose wheel doors so I could open them to get more of a draft and keep the fumes down to a minimum. The doors were stuck, and I had to kick them open. I also cracked the bomb bay doors, and had the gunners remove the waist windows. We flew out over the Adriatic and I helped the bombardier release the bombs by hand in the open bomb bay. We came back and landed O.K. I wonder how long out luck will hold out. PS We're scheduled for a mission tomorrow.

376th Bomb Group, Mission No. 392, December 28, 1944

Mission status:

- Target: Bressanone, Italy; railroad bridge
- Crew points: 2 sorties, 1 mission.
- Flight time: 5:45 hours
- Target distance: Approx. 532 miles (884)

Flight leaders:

- A Flight: Col. Snyder, Capt. Miller (512th Squadron)
- B Flight: Lt. Smith (513th Squadron)

Flight box configuration:

Capt. Miller		A	
Lt. Witkin	B	C	Lt. Smith
Capt. Albrecht		D	

Aircraft statistics:

- Aircraft at takeoff: 26
- Aircraft over target: 25
- Aircraft returned to base: 26
- Aircraft diverted or forced landing: 0

Mission summary:

- Bomb load: 134 1,000-lb bombs

- Anti-aircraft: Heavy but scant and inaccurate

- Fighter escort: None

- Bombing results: Satisfactory. Approaches made 800 ft. south of bridge and three direct hits were made on the bridge.

- Mission commentary: Again, our crew and plane flew as a filler crew. Col. Snyder and Capt. Miller were the leaders for the 512th and Lt. Smith lead the 513th Squadron.

> **Paul's diary:** We went after another bridge in Brenner Pass today. The weather was clear and cold. We had a flight alert as soon as we hit Northern Italy. If they were there, they didn't show themselves or try to make a pass at us. The target (a railroad bridge) was visible. We are sure we knocked it out. Tail gunner fired on an unidentified B-24 who joined our box on the bomb run. This ship was later found to be one out of our group. They shot a lot of flak up at us, but we dropped bombs and turned off course just before we came in range of it. This was a pretty easy mission. Hope to see more like it.
> P. S. We are going out again tomorrow.

376th Bomb Group, Mission 393, December 29, 1944

Mission status:

- Target: Bressanone, Italy; railroad bridge

- Crew points: 2 sorties, 1 mission

- Flight time: 5:45 hours

- Target distance: Approx. 532 miles (884 km)

Flight leaders:

- A Flight: Maj. Kornrumph, Capt. McChesney (513th Squadron)
- B Flight: Lt. Pelzaman (514th Squadron)

Flight box configuration:

Capt. McChesney	A		
Lt. Pelzman	B	C	Lt. Clark
Lt. Carlson	D		

Aircraft statistics:

- Aircraft at takeoff: 27
- Aircraft over target: 27
- Aircraft returned to base: 26
- Aircraft diverted or forced landing: 1
- Aircraft lost: 1
- Aircraft damage: 5 major, 1 minor due to anti-aircraft

Mission summary:

- Bomb load: 145 1,000-lb bombs
- Casualties: One seriously wounded airman, one lightly wounded
- Bombing results: Superior. Dropped 72 % of our bombs on and around bridge and within 1,000 ft.
- Fighter escort: P-51s flew protection and escort mission
- Anti-aircraft: Heavy to moderate and accurate

- Mission commentary: This was the third strike at the same target in as many days.

> **Paul's diary:** Today is a day the whole crew will remember. We had our first flak casualty. Andy Duval, the Sperry ball gunner got a bad wound in his left foot. Flak came up through the floor, ripped out part of his foot, and went out through the top. He has a bad flesh wound and a compound fracture. He's going to be O.K., but will be in the hospital for a good while.
>
> The target was another bridge in Brenner Pass and they really shot hell out of us, but we didn't lose a ship. Flak came through the windshield right in my face, but by a miracle, it missed all three of us—pilot, copilot, and myself; although Bill, the copilot, got glass from the windshield in one of his eyes. We saw ME 109s just as we came out of the Alps and hit the Adriatic, but for some reason, they didn't come in on us.

> *Author's note: A comment from Mike Ozkcus seems appropriate here: "Years ago a man, with whom I worked, went to Europe for a vacation. He did the whole tourist bit and was amazed at all the modern transportation (railroads, fast commuter trains, etc.) and how superior they were to our deteriorated railroads. I explained to him that during the war we destroyed any form of transportation, if it moved, was going to move, or was planning to move. So the Europeans have us to thank for their great new transportation system."*

10

A Quiet Time for Crew 313: January 1945

A mission over the Ploesti Oil Refinery in Ploesti, Romania

A Mix of Events
By Emmett (Mac) MacKenzie

After the experiences of December 27th, 28th, and 29th, it was with sheer relief that our crew was not scheduled to fly for a while. Only six missions were to be flown by the 376th in January. Luckily, we were not scheduled to fly any of those missions.

On January 8, 1945, the 395th mission had been scheduled. It was the second mission to be flown in January. The target was Lenz, Austria. Lenz was a few miles inside of the Austrian boarder with Italy. It was a bad target to hit; just a railroad-marshaling yard nestled in a narrow valley between two mountains on each side. The yard was like a bowling alley with no gutters on either side; just a straight and narrow corridor with an entrance and an exit. It bristled with anti-aircraft guns that couldn't miss their target, not even if the German and Austrian gunners were blindfolded.

On the same day as the mission, there was a big rush to enhance the physical appearance of the "main street" of the 514th Squadron. How could the appearance of a dusty conclave of three, squat, one-story Tufa-block buildings and a big and dusty mess tent be improved? The first building housed the squadron headquarters and a mailroom. The second building was used for briefings and debriefings of crews. The third building was used to house the parachute inspection tables and the airmen's flight equipment such as heated flying suits and flak vests. However, one piece of equipment that never left the plane was the flak helmets. They were always left in the planes because of eccentric value—zero except when used over the target area.

Word was sent out from the 376th headquarters to spruce up Main Street. It had to look like a small hometown with a well-kept parkway. But who cared what the street look liked, certainly not the enlisted men! However, the enlisted men were delegated the task and were told that the squadron was to be inspected by a highly placed general from the 15th Air Force Headquarters. We were delegated the responsibility for giving the street a face lift. And, literally speaking, that's what we did. Any clutter along the street was hauled away. At the same time truckloads of enlisted men were sent out to scour the countryside for evergreen trees. It wasn't long before we found enough trees to satisfy the operations officer. The trees were brought back to the base and planted at measured intervals along Main Street in front of Squadron Headquarters, the parachute building, the mess hall, etc. To the casual observer, one may have thought we were rushing Arbor Day by about two months. After all the work was done and the area had been "beautified," the effort and the expenditure of energy were questionable because the inspection was called off. More pressing matters had probably confronted the general. Personally, I was glad to be working on the ground rather than to be flying.

But returning to the mission, it was to have been an "all-out" mission. In fact, several days before the mission was to be flown, maintenance personnel were working furiously to make flyable an un-flyable plane located in the repair shop area. It had no landing gear, oxygen system, or gun emplacements. It had been stripped down and scavenged for parts to be used so that other planes might fly. But this time, the aircraft mechanics had to find and install this plane's missing equipment. The airmen would never know where the parts had come from. Miraculously, the plane was made flyable over a very short time and was to be one of thirteen planes to be flown that day. The mission turned out to be a very costly one. On this day, not one of our squadron's planes returned to base. How could anyone not remember such a fateful day? The planting project forever reminded me of the loss of our planes. A sense of relief swept over our crew, having not been assigned to fly this mission. We were happy to be allowed to dig up and plant trees all along Main Street.

Normally our squadron's planes began returning from their mission about 1530 to 1700 hours (3:30 to 5:00 pm), depending on the distance flown. On this day, landings would be later because Lenz was approximately 667 miles (1,073 km) from San Pangrazio. Because this mission was such a big deal, some of our crew decided to watch for the returning planes to land. We waited and watched for the planes from the

514th to land. Our viewpoint was from our tent site. There was no sound of engines being throttled back prior to landing. No sound of the landing gear clanking into the locked-down position, or tires making skittish noises as the wheels touched the runway. Nothing was heard! Our wait began late in the afternoon and continued until dark. Not one plane had landed during this time. Something had gone very wrong. Finally we gave up waiting, went to chow, and returned to our tent wondering what had happened.

The next day we learned that what we had suspected had happening. It wasn't a question of whether or not all the planes had been shot down and lost. It was a combination of events. Undoubtedly, some planes had been shot down; others may have been forced to land in unfriendly territory such as Croatia, Yugoslavia, while other planes had been diverted to bases farther up the Italian boot because of the severe damage inflicted on them. To top this all off, the weather in Southern Europe was lousy during the whole month of January. It was cold, cloudy, and windy with just a touch of snow.

To validate this event, Paul's diary notes, Roy's notes, and my Form 5 records show that we flew no missions between January and February 1st. Normally we flew four or five sorties/missions each month. A stand-down of this nature by our crew was not normal. Even Robert James, the maintenance officer in the 512th, had a vague recollection of our stand-down. However there is one bit of contradictory evidence. Official records indicate that two missions had been flown on January 15th and on the 31st, which included the 514th Squadron. I do not know how to reconcile these records with what I believed to have happened except for the possibility that some 514th crews had flown with other squadrons.

Another bit of interesting information relating to this event is my vivid recollection that our squadron did not fly until we had received war-weary replacement B-24s from the 8th Air Force. They were old and battered planes with many hours logged on their engines and many missions under their wings. They had been flown out of England into the heart of Germany in 1944 prior to the winding down of the Southern European Theatre. Among the number was the famous "Boomerang," in which we as a crew flew several times. True to its name, Boomerang always found its way back to base. By April the plane had flown 125 missions, a feat which was unheard of in those days. Soon after, it was retired and flown back to the U.S. and put on display in numerous cities for people to see.

Targets and Related War Stories
By Mike Ozkcus

This is just an aside story that might be considered funny. My copilot in the Army Transport Command was shot down behind enemy lines during the invasion of southern France. The peasants, not the partisans, got to him and hid him in an outhouse. He stayed there three days while the peasants used the outhouse and brought him food. They couldn't understand each other because of the language barrier. The best and only thing that he could do for himself was to crack the door open and get some fresh air occasionally. After three days he heard the voice of American GIs and stepped out of the outhouse to fresh air and freedom.

The Landmark

We hit Salzburg, Austria several times. It never was much of a deal. We usually came out of the raids in pretty good shape. However, there are a couple of instances that remain in my memory. On one flight coming back from a raid, I became confused. It had been under-cast for some time and I could not pick up accurate figures to pinpoint our position. Unexpectedly, there came a burst of flak. I knew immediately that we were over Salzburg. That burst of flak gave me all the information that I needed to know. Someone on our crew asked, "What was that?" I just said, Salzburg. From there we headed home. Months later, we were partying at a rest camp on the Isle of Capri. Paul O'Steen kept building me up about what a great navigator I was, and then he said, except for that one time over Salzburg. I never told anyone what a big help Salzburg was to me that day.

The Mickey Man and Steering Clear

Toward the end of the war, the Air Force started putting radar equipment in the planes that were designated as the "Lead planes". The plane's Sperry ball-belly turret was removed and replaced with the radar electronic unit. Radar works on the relative reflectivity of various materials. For example, water appears dark on the screen. A town or a city will appear lighter than the land. A coastline on the radarscope would show the same as a map except one would be in shades of black and white, while the map would be in pretty colors. The radar picture was so clear that it was possible to bomb through the under-cast and expect to hit the target. This was my understanding at the time I was introduced to radar.

Along with radar came the operator who we called the "Mickey Man." He was a navigator who was also trained in radar. The navigator in the nose was still in charge. Mickey sat on the flight deck with his navigation equipment. Life was much more simplified for the crew's navigator. Instead of constantly taking readings and figuring on his E-6B hand-held mechanical computer device, now all he had to do was to ask Mickey for a bearing or a fix. In less time than it takes to write about it, Mickey would give a bearing from a certain spot plus a distance. Placing this information on your map would locate your exact position. A man could learn to love work like that navigator.

I still kept navigating on my own, keeping track of the plane's flight with occasional fixes from Mickey. On one mission, we were on a bomb run to hit Salzburg (I don't remember whether it was our primary or secondary target). Bombing through a completely under-cast condition using radar, Mickey made navigation all very dramatic. He kept calling out the heading, the correction he was making, and the time to "bombs-away." This bomb run was a piece of cake until it dawned on me just before we were to drop the bombs that there was no flak, which was not like Salzburg. I looked out of the plane at 3:00

o'clock, the right side of the plane. There was a break in the clouds and there was Salzburg, 20 to 30 miles to the right of our bomb run. We were way off target. At "bombs-away," I gave a heading home and decided that we had a very poor Mickey or a very smart one who flew a very safe bomb run. After that I made sure to compile my own figures when I flew with a Mickey Radarman.

The following story by Joe Aberwald appeared in the Stars and Stripes in January 1945. It adds to the Christmas Day story:

Lady Luck Rides with "Boomerang" as She "Sweats Out" Rotation 376th Bomb Group (PRO)

Lady Luck once more intervened last week, aiding Liberandos Boomerang, 514th Squadron B-24, to boost its string of missions to 123 and tie an Air Force record for heavy bombers. While over Brenner Pass Wednesday, another Liberator went out of control and collided its front belly surface with the rudder and vertical stabilizer of the famous Boomerang, rendering them useless. Exercising all skills, Lt. Robert Robertson, pilot, kept Boomerang under control and waded through thick flak, which knocked out the No. 1 engine and demolished the vacuum system. Despite the serious damage, Lt. Robertson succeeded in flying the plane back to the 376th base. Tension is mounting as the Liberator nears the 125th mission mark. Sgt. J. R. Cochran, radio operator, who finished his present tour in Liberandos Boomerang on this, its most precarious mission, remarked. "A lot of missions have had me worried but this one topped them all. Maybe I'm wrong, but I believe Liberandos-Boomerang will be returned to the United States as the holder of the greatest record ever established by heavy bombardment aircraft." It now has 123 missions, the last 89 without a turn-back due to mechanical failure." Doing its part to carry Christmas presents to Hitler, Liberandos-Boomerang participated in the Christmas day attack on Hall, Austria.

Crew 313 participated in the following missions 376th Bomb Group, Mission No. 395, January 8, 1945

Mission status:

- Target: Lenz, Austria; North main railroad marshalling yard
- Crew points: 0 sortie and 0 mission
- Flight time: 8:30 hours
- Target distance: 520 miles (837km)

Flight leaders:

- A Flight: Maj. Wimberley, Lt. Andrew (515th Squadron)
- B Flight: Capt. Albrecht (514th Squadron)

Mission box configuration: Not available

Aircraft statistics:

- Aircraft at takeoff: 28
- Aircraft over target: 23
- Aircraft returned to base: 26
- Aircraft diverted or forced landing: 1
- Aircraft lost: 1 destroyed, mechanical
- Aircraft damage: 5 major, 1 minor due to anti-aircraft

Mission summary:

- Bomb load: 163 500-lb bombs

- Anti-aircraft: Heavy to moderate and inaccurate
- Airmen casualties: 4 killed, 7 seriously wounded
- Fighter escort: 50 P-51s and 6 P-38s
- Mission commentary: Unable to observe results due to weather. Path Finder Fix operators reported good run.

11

Missions Increase: February 1945

The Patriotic Thing to Do
By Emmett (Mac) MacKenzie

Between 1941 and 1945, much social engineering was done on the home front as well as in the military itself to design, develop, and implement the intended and forthcoming military effort. "Patriotism" was the foremost ideological concept to be set before all Americans by the U.S. Government. It mattered not so much as what was done on the part of families or individuals as it was the fact that Americans, if not working on the military production line or serving in the armed forces, must in some small measure demonstrate their patriotism and contribute to the war effort. To this end, the idea of "recycling" cooking oils and worn out products on a grand scale, first came into being. Grease from home cooking, aluminum cooking utensils, metal lipstick tube holders, and worn out old tires all were to be turned into government depots for recycling.

Financing the war effort was another major concern for the government. To address this problem, Congress authorized the sale of savings bonds. Again, patriotism became the key word. All Americans were encouraged to participate, and they did, civilians along with military personnel. The purchase of U.S. Class-E Saving Bonds was a drive in which all squadrons of the 376th Bomb Group were encouraged to participate. The cost of the saving bonds purchased was deducted from the monthly pay that each man received. The airmen generally sent the certificate of purchase home just as a safety precaution.

One special drive was the "Great E-Bond Drive." A contest was devised which would challenge each crew in every squadron of the 376th Bomb Group. The crew that bought the most bonds would be the recipients of the reward. Our crew purchased the greatest numbers of E-Bonds and was to be rewarded a free sight-seeing trip to Rome for one week. I remember our crew coming together and agreeing to make large monthly purchases of the infamous E-Bonds. After a period of time, and having more important things on our minds than savings bonds, our crew was informed that we had won the coveted grand prize. We were all filled with the pride of our accomplishment and elated with the prospect of going to Rome. What a great week that would be! But fate was to introduce a new twist to the turn of events. Because Rome could not accommodate so many military personnel and there were very limited accommodations for enlisted men, the enlisted men were excluded from receiving this grand prize. It was a bruising blow to the men's collective efforts. They had planned to have a grand time, and now it was not to be. It didn't seem fair. Was all the planning and effort for naught? The experience once again raised the age-old question of "what is fair in love or war." On reflection, I believe we soon realized that this event was not the end of the world. We were still alive, well, and would continue to fly until we had reached the magic number of 50 missions at which point we would be rotated states-side. In some small way, our crew had contributed to the "Great American and Allied World War Two Victory."

It wasn't until late January 1945 that we started flying again. Prior to this time, our days were filled with practice flights. During off hours, crewmembers visited the local towns of San Pangrazio, Manduria, Lecci, etc. We bartered with the local merchants to make "Eisenhower Jackets" (Air Corps. approved) out of our newly acquired long coat, "dress greens." Jim Snell, our top turret gunner, tutored an Italian student whose family washed our clothes. There was plenty of time for every one to write letters home to their wives, girl friends, and parents. Some squadron duties were to be expected, but in general, we probably did quite a bit of just plain goofing off.

The Home Construction Business

Local military ground personnel and Italian entrepreneurs got together and formed a home construction business in the 514th Squadron. Our crew's enlisted men had talked to other squadron personnel about the houses that they had had local contractors built for them. The ground personnel were the general contractors and the local Italians did the actual construction. The Americans who had access to local suppliers purchased wood, glass, and Tufa building blocks.

Many of the ground crews were living in these relatively luxurious accommodations. After all, they were the "long timers" and they deserved all the comforts of a home. But, didn't we all deserve a better place to live? A cold and drafty tent wasn't our crew's idea of a desired living space. As a result, the building bug bit our crew.

The price of the home depended on what options the customer wanted, i.e. the number of rooms (generally two), the number of windows, and the possibility of a chimney or fireplace. The architectural features of this building were certainly simplistic; rectangular in shape with corrugated sheets resting on a wooden-gable-roof frame.

So at long last, we entered into serious discussions with the contractors. As a crew, we decided on what we thought was an acceptable plan to meet our requirements. The cost? A mere $1,900 American dollars. The amount of money was not so difficult to part with, but when the G.I. contractor-builders said it would be at least four-to-six months before they could build our "dream" home, we got cold feet and decided against this venture. After all was said and done, we had no idea of how long we would be in the squadron before we met the 50-mission requirement necessary for rotation back to the states. As it turned out, the decision not to build was one of the smartest decisions our crew ever made. We continued to live in our 12 by 12, Government Issued, pyramid tent that came quipped with four-foot, flap-type vertical sides, a wooden front door entrance, and free air conditioning. We lived there until when we were told we had to move out.

Fortunes Favorites
By Emmett (Mac) MacKenzie with the recollections of Roy Hatem, Jim Snell, and Paul O'Steen

The months of February and March undoubtedly encapsulated some of the most harrowing experiences that our crew ever lived through. The following mission incidents occurred while we attempted to achieve the magic numbers of 50 missions, which would allow our crew to return stateside. We had just resumed flying again on February 1st after almost a month of being grounded. The actions taken by individual crew members merit inclusion in our crew's history because they exemplify the cohesiveness, loyalty, and the concern for each other's welfare.

The Hazards of Defusing Bombs

If we couldn't drop our bombs because clouds obscured the target and we had no plane that had the "Mickey Radar" navigational equipment, it was standard operation procedure to defuse the bomb load before returning to base. Defusing the bomb load was a very common practice. Guy Bretilotte, our bombardier, had done it successfully many times before. On this particular occasion when Roy told Guy to go back to the bomb bay and defuse the bombs. Paul was to assist Guy. It was not unusual for the metal components to freeze up because of the intense cold (40 to 60 degrees below zero). This happened to be one of those days. Guy, with his insulated leather gloves covering his hands, was working furiously with his fuse wrench in an attempt to unscrew the fuses from the bombs—all to no avail. When the fuse did not respond to muscle power, Guy resorted to tapping the fuse with his fuse wrench. When this effort didn't produce the desired results, he began to attack the fuse more forcefully. He knew the bombs had to be defused before returning to base but the cores would not budge. Added to his discomfort was the fact that he and Paul had to breath through their oxygen masks, which were attached to small portable oxygen bottles that were good for a half hour at the most.

There probably was no real danger, but Guy's actions drove Paul up the sides of the bomb bay walls, figuratively speaking. He was really fearful as to what might happen. Out of concern for Guy and the crew, Paul told me that he left the bomb bay and hurriedly returned to the flight deck and told Roy about the problem. Roy went right to the scene. What transpired between himself and Guy only the two know. Probably the solution was to wait until the plane reached a lower altitude where the fuses could be more easily unscrewed and the bombs defused.

Preparedness and Luck are the Keys to Survival

Everyone knew that a B-24 could easily return to base with just three engines operating or, for that matter, two engines if the aircraft was properly flown. Flight with two engines is manageable, but flight with one operating engine, now that was a real chore.

As Roy acquired more flying skills under combat conditions, the question of how to handle a B-24 with one engine became more crucial in his thinking. He knew the B-24 could be flown back to base with two engines. He had done this before under combat conditions and in B-24 Flight Training School. To quote Roy, "But what if the situation arises and I've got to fly this boxcar with just one engine? How do I do it? How long can we stay aloft?" He was about to find the answers to his questions.

Flight training was not something crews did only while stationed states-side. It had its place in the 514th Squadron also. Sometimes the training included only the pilot, copilot, and the flight engineer. On this particular day, Capt. Edward S. Reno, the 514th's Operational Officer, invited Roy to fly a practice mission with him, each man with his own three-man crew and plane. Roy was to follow Reno's lead in cutting power to the engines while maintaining control of the plane. Having become airborne and reached a satisfactory altitude for executing these particular flight maneuvers, Capt. Reno told Roy to follow his lead. First, Reno cut out one of his four engines. Roy followed suit. Reno cut out two engines, so did Roy. Reno cut out three engines and Roy did the same proving that good flight control could still be maintained. Finally, Reno cut out all four engines. So did Roy, allowing his plane to glide on past the time that Reno had started up his engines again. That was the day that Roy realized and was confident that the B-24 was a very stable flying machine and had good gliding characteristics. Detractors of the plane and its design said that the plane would fly like a rock if anything happened to it engines. This was not true. The narrow cross-section of the plane's Davis wing did not keep it from soaring like a big bird with a 110-foot wingspan.

After landing, parking their planes, and waiting for a Jeep to return the two crews to squadron headquarters, Reno smiled slightly and said, "That was a good practice flight, wasn't it?" Roy nodded and acknowledged his acceptance as a first rate pilot.

With all the acquired flying techniques in toe, Roy mentally filed away all the above-acquired knowledge for some possible rainy day when it might be needed. It was Roy's self-imposed philosophy to train himself to the best of his ability and to make sure that the crew cross-trained in some other member's military occupational specialty (MOS). The motto that Roy lived by, insisting that the crew do likewise, was "be prepared." In retrospect, it was this motto that gave us a staying presence in the 514th Squadron. Ours was a crew that would see its missions through and return home safely.

A test of Roy's preparedness probably occurred on the February 13 mission to Zagreb. Our crew was the lead crew for the 514th Squadron. It was on this mission, as Roy recalls it, that "I was forced to draw on all my skills acquired in training, in combat, and in my private thought scenarios. What do I do if this or that happens?" Our Target was the city's railroad marshalling yards. It was a visual target and the flak was accurate and heavy. We lost one engine from flak on the bomb run. "I told Bill to cut the power to the lost engine and to feather its prop," Roy explained. Feathering the prop involved shutting down the engine and orientating the three bladed propellers with hydraulic fluid pressure so that the blades cut directly into the air stream like a knife. We continued flying toward our base using the remaining three engines. "Not long after the first incident, we experienced a runaway prop on a second engine. Bill tried to keep the prop under control by feathering and unfeathering the prop blades in an attempt to keep the engine with in the prescribed limits of operation. Bill was unable to do this, as the engine would not respond to this type of coaxing. Then Bill cut the power to the second engine and feathered the prop. This left us flying on two engines. We could not lead our box formation and had to drop out of formation. We gradually lost altitude but maintained complete control."

Roy continued his story. "Before we could get to the Adriatic Sea, we had to cross a high mountain range near the coast of Yugoslavia. It was obvious that the two good engines did not have the power to lift the plane high enough to clear the mountain ridge in front of us. The only choice left was to attempt to restart the engine with the runaway prop and hope that the engine would last long enough to give us enough power to get us over the ridge. So Bill un-freathered the engine and we prayed. Luckily, it worked and our plane headed for the Adriatic. It was my decision to use the three engines as long as the runaway prop did not act up again. Unfortunately, we had a runaway prop again after we reached the Adriatic, this time on the third engine. Once again, Bill feathered it and we proceeded home on two engines. Having approached the runway, I aligned the plane with it and made the final approach, but then one of the two remaining engines began to falter. Rather than risk its loss on the landing approach, I shut down both remaining engines and landed the plane with no power. If the faltering engine had failed at the last minute, the one remaining good engine would have pulled the plane across and off the runway causing a possible a crash landing." Once again, we returned safely back to base.

Paul's Job: Keep Those Guys in the "Coffin Seats" Covered

In his diary, Paul does not mention the following incident but he related it to me. The story relates to the hazards of piloting the "big bird." The pilots' seats were deep, carved-out seats constructed of steel or thick aluminum that encased the pilots and protected them totally on the back, and partially on the sides from flak—hence the name "coffin seats." On this mission, Paul was standing in his position located between the two pilots ready to respond to any order from the pilots. Additionally, Paul monitored the fuel gauges for the wing tanks. If fuel had to be transferred from a reserve tank to a wing tank of a particular engine, Paul was the man to do it.

As our plane headed down the bomb run, a heavy barrage of flak surrounded our box formation. Roy turned to look out the pilot's bubble window on the left side. As usual, his flak helmet restricted his view and kept getting in his way. Solution—take the dammed thing off. At that same brief moment, Paul looked over at Roy and seeing that he didn't have his flak helmet on, he grabbed Roy's helmet and jammed it on Roy's head. Right then, a piece of flak hit the windshield and showered both Roy and Bill with small sharp shards of plastic. Luckily, neither one was seriously injured. Paul had responded above and beyond his duty to protect the plane and its crew.

The Oxygen Connection

It was another one of those dateless missions in which all seemed to be going well. On this occasion, Guy, had gone back to the waist looking for a place to stretch out and relax before assuming his duties as the crew's bombardier. The initial turning point (IP), the point from which we turned to initiate the bombing run, were still a long way off, but Mike continually checked his navigational charts, plotted the course, and maintained our location. He was meticulous to a fault and made certain at all times that he knew the location of the squadron formation as well as that of our own plane. One never knew when foul weather over the Alps might be responsible for the squadron or group commanders to issue an order to "break-off-mission" order and return to base. It was SOP (Standard Operational Procedure) that every navigator be responsible at all times to know his plane's exact location so, if necessary, he could direct the plane and its crew safely to base.

For some reason or other, maybe it was fate, I had stayed in the nose of the plane. I probably wanted to see the landscape below our plane. Whatever the reason, my presence in the nose was a fortuitous situation. Roy was talking to Mike, probably asking about our position as the engines of the plane droned noisily on. Since that the discussion was between Roy and Mike, I didn't pay any attention. However, because of the plane's elevation, the whole crew was on oxygen. At some point in the intercom discussion, Roy seemed to be talking to himself and was not able to get a response from Mike. Then Roy yelled out, "Mac, what the hell is going on up there. I can't raise Mike. Mac, get out of your turret and see if his he's plugged into the intercom." Turning my attention to Mike, he appeared to be leaning over his navigation table working. First I checked his intercom connection and I told Roy it was OK. Instantaneously, Roy said, "I still can't get Mike to respond. Check his oxygen." I checked it and discovered Mike was not getting any oxygen. His oxygen line was lying on the deck detached from the oxygen system. He was losing consciousness. At twenty thousand feet, it doesn't take long to pass out due to lack of oxygen. I quickly plugged his line into the system and he started coming around. I asked if he was OK and he said that he was and then he resumed his discussion with Roy at the point where he had left off. After only a few minutes had elapsed, once again Mike stopped responding coherently.

I check his line again and discovered it had again become detached, so I plugged his line into the system a second time. This same scenario repeated itself at least one more time before I could secure his line permanently.

In August 1993, Mike reminded me of this event. I hadn't thought about it since it had happened forty-nine years earlier. Truly, we were "fortunes favorites," as Gaius Marius Caesar of Roman history would have proclaimed. Romans were great believers in preparedness, luck, and fate.

Ol' Boomerang and Her Ignoble End

I had the impression that it was February when we first flew in Ol' Boomerang, the famous plane that had come to us as a transplant from England, but Roy remembers that the squadron acquired her from States-side early on during the war. True to her name though, she always returned to the 514th Squadron regardless of what crew was flying her. Those crews who flew her had proven track records and ours was one of them. Years later during my last talk with Jim on October 6th, 1994, he told me of a casual discussion between two 461st Heavy Bombing Group men at their reunion. These two guys were talking about B-24s and one of them told the other that he had flown on a rather famous B-24, Ol' Boomerang. He said he would sure like to know what happened to her. The second guy said, "Oh I know what happened to her! She was sent to a salvage yard and I was that guy that cut her up for scrap metal." What a fate for such a gallant old war bird. She deserved better, but her accomplishments will live on so long as there are crews to remember her.

Crew 313 participated in the following missions 376th Bomb Group, Mission No. 400, February 1, 1945

Mission status:

- Target: Vienna, Austria, Moosbierbaum Oil Refinery
- Crew points: 0 sorties, 0 mission
- Total flight time: 6:40 hours
- Distance to target: 482 miles (801 km)

Aircraft statistics:

- Aircraft at takeoff: 31
- Aircraft over target: 0
- Aircraft returned to base: 29
- Aircraft diverted or forced landing: 2

Flight leaders:

- A Flight: Col. Graff, Capt. Turner (512th Squadron)
- B Flight: Lt. Smith (514th Squadron)

Flight box configuration:

Capt. Turner	A		
Maj. Mansel	B	C	Lt. Smith
Capt. McChesney	D		

Mission summary:

- Bomb load: 219 500-lb bombs
- Anti-aircraft: Heavy, scant, and inaccurate
- Bombing results: No bombs dropped

> **Paul's diary:** Today was our first mission in thirty days. We went to Vienna but couldn't bomb as we ran into some very bad weather and had to turn back. We hit some light but accurate flak in German-held Yugoslavia, but they didn't hit any of our planes.

376th Bomb Group Mission No. 401, December 2, 1945

Mission status:

- Target: Salzburg, Austria; railroad marshalling yard
- Crew points: 0 sorties, 0 mission
- Total flight time: 6:40 hours
- Distance to target: 482 miles (801 km)

Flight leaders:

- A Flight: Capt. Dale (515th Squadron)
- B Flight: Capt. Roeca

Flight box configuration:

Capt. Dale   A

Capt. Carlson   B   C   Capt. Roeca

Lt. Nemitz   D

Aircraft statistics:

- Aircraft at takeoff: 31
- Aircraft over target: 29
- Aircraft returned to base: 32
- Aircraft diverted or forced landing: 0

Mission summary:

- Bomb load: 221 500-lb bombs
- Bombing results: Bombs hit in river and fields at least 3,600' from objective
- Anti-aircraft: Heavy, scant, and inaccurate
- Fighter escort: 36 P-51s
- Mission commentary: The mission was lead by Maj. Wimberley of the 515th Squadron. No other squadron was recorded as having flown. The 514th Squadron was not included in the official records as having flown but Roy and Mac's Form 5 Records indicate that we did fly as a crew that day.

> **Paul's diary:** Went to Salzburg, Austria today. Flew lead ship in our box. Not much to tell about on this mission. The flak wasn't too bad, but was accurate as hell.

376th Bomb Group, Mission No. 407, February 13, 1945

Mission status:

- Target: Zagreb, Yugoslavia; railroad marshalling yards
- Flight time: 6:00 hours
- Target distance: Approx. 352 miles (571 km)
- Crew points: 2 sorties, 1 mission

Flight leaders:

- A Flight: Col. Snyder, Capt Fuller (513th Squadron)
- B Flight: Lt. Hatem (514th Squadron)
- C Flight: Lt. Davis (515th Squadron)

Aircraft statistics:

- Aircraft at takeoff: 19
- Aircraft over target: 19
- Aircraft diverted or forced landing: 0
- Aircraft lost: 2 destroyed
- Aircraft damaged: 2 major, 1 (anti-aircraft)

Mission summary:

- Bomb load: 145 500-lb bombs
- Bomb results: Good concentration on target. Two explosions reported in marshalling yards and several fires. Bombing by Path Finder Fix.

> **Paul's diary:** Today we went to Zagreb, Yugoslavia. Bombed the railroad marshalling yard. It was our first mission flying lead. Target was visual and the flak was heavy and accurate. All the planes in our box were hit, but all came back O.K.

376th Bomb Group, Mission No. 411, February 17, 1945

Mission status:

Target: Graz, Austria; railroad marshalling yard
Crew points: 2 sorties, 1 mission
Flight time: 8:30 hours
Target distance: Approx. 436 miles (707 km)

Aircraft statistics:

- Aircraft at takeoff: 29

- Aircraft over target: 28

- Aircraft returned to base: 28

- Aircraft diverted or forced landing: 1

- Aircraft lost: 0

- Aircraft damaged: 1 major (anti-aircraft), 1 major (mechanical failure)

Airmen casualties:

- Killed: 2

- Wounded: 1 seriously

Flight leaders:

- A Flight: Capt. Bishop (515th Squadron)
- B Flight: Lt. Shawberger (512th Squadron)
- C Flight: Lt. Hatem (514th Squadron)

Mission summary:

- Bomb load: 214 500-lb bombs
- Navigational Aid/Bombing: Path Finder Fix
- Fighter escort: 40 P-51s
- Mission commentary: Missed the target but hit a chemical plant. No camera coverage.

> **Paul's diary:** Our mission today was the Tiger Tank Works at Lenz, Austria. We ran into a solid under-cast over the continent so we dropped our bombs by radar. We had a fighter alert, but saw no enemy planes. We had a P-51 escort and it was really swell to see them flying around us.

> *Author's comment: If our crew had flown as indicated by Paul's diary, the target would have been the Tiger Tank Works in Lenz, Austria. My Form 5 record indicates no mission flown on this date. I was on sick leave in Lecci, Italy.*

376th Bomb Group, Mission No. 415, February 22, 1945

Mission status:

- Target: Newmarkt, Germany

- Crew points: 2 sorties, 1 mission
- Flight time: 8:30 hours
- Target distance: Approx. 627 miles (1,003 km)

Aircraft statistics:

- Aircraft at takeoff: 31
- Aircraft over target: 30
- Aircraft returned to base: 30
- Aircraft diverted or forced landing: 1

Flight leaders:

- A Flight: Maj. Kornrummph, Capt. McKenzie (512th Squadron)
- B Flight: Maj. Mansell (515th Squadron)
- C Flight: Capt. Hatem (514th Squadron)
- D Flight: Maj. Hoover (513th Squadron)

Mission summary:

- Bomb load: 163 500-lb bombs
- Bomb results: Smoke and cloud covered prevented accurate observation
- Fighter escort: 50 P-38s and P 51s
- Anti-aircraft: Heavy, moderate, and inaccurate.
- Mission commentary: Attempts to hit alternate target. The target was the greatest distance we had ever flown or would ever fly.

> **Paul's diary:** Today our mission was a railroad marshalling yard deep into Germany. Over the target we ran into a thick haze so we could not drop our bombs. We started home and were fired on at Salzburg, Austria. All planes came out O.K. so we dropped our bombs on a small town in the Austrian Alps.

376th Bomb Group, Mission No. 417, February 24, 1945

Mission status:

- Target: Verona, Italy; locomotive shop and railroad marshalling yards
- Crew points: 2 sorties, 1 mission
- Target distance: Approx. 470 miles (752 km)
- Flying time: 4:00 hours

Aircraft statistics:

- Aircraft at takeoff: 26
- Aircraft over target: 24
- Aircraft returned to base: 25
- Aircraft diverted or forced landing: 1
- Aircraft damaged: 2 major (anti-aircraft)
- Aircraft damaged: 2 major, 1 (anti-aircraft), 3 minor

Flight leaders:

- A Flight: Maj. Kornrummph, Capt. Kemp (512th Squadron)

- B Flight: Lt. Taqnvas (515th Squadron)
- C Flight: Lt. Pelsman (513th Squadron)
- D Flight: Lt. Lt. Doty (513th Squadron)

Mission summary:

- Bomb load: 147 500-lb bombs
- Bomb results: Very satisfactory
- Anti-aircraft: Heavy, scant, and accurate
- Fighter escort: 25 P-51s
- Mission commentary: A lot of track was torn up, repair shops hit, and much of the rolling stock was destroyed.

376th Bomb Group, Mission No. 418
February 25, 1945

Flight leaders:

- A Flight: Col. George, Lt. Hoover (513th Squadron)
- B Flight: Lt. Hatem (514th Squadron)
- C Flight: Capt. Dale (515th Squadron)
- D Flight: Lt. Sossaman (512th Squadron)

Mission summary:

- Bomb load: 181 500-lb bombs
- Bomb results: All units overshot or undershot target. Smoke prevented observation.
- Anti-aircraft: Heavy, intense, and accurate

- Navigational aid/bombing: Path Finder Fix
- Fighter escort: 50 P-51s

> **Paul's diary:** Today we went to Lenz, Austria. This is one of the toughest targets we have so we all sweated it out, and with a good reason. There was a solid cloud of it about a mile in length and spread right across the target, which was the railroad marshalling yard. They tracked us all the way down the bomb run and God only knows why they didn't get at least half of us. The tail gunner (Byron) got hit in the side with a piece, but his flak suit stopped the piece and, without a doubt, saved his life. I'll never forget that bomb run, and hope I never see another like it.

> *Author's comment: There is at least one discrepancy between the official 376th Heavy Bombardment Group records and the missions as described in Paul's diary. The reader should only view these differences in the light of human frailties rather than to assign error to a particular source.*

12

Memories and Reflections: March 1945

Weary flight crew returning to base after a mission

The words of Colonel Henry Taylor, 514th Squadron Commander

> *Author's comment: I had a pleasant conversation with Henry Taylor at our September 1994 reunion and have corresponded with him since. In one of our conversations, I asked him if he would write an article for our crew's Newsletter. He said he would be pleased to write down a few of his recollections of serving in the 514th Bomb Squadron. I am personally grateful to him for agreeing to contribute to our newsletter, which would serve to enhance our memories of those days some fifty years ago. I offered a couple of ideas and Henry said "I'll do that and sort of go on from there with a rambling style of things I remember, which you may find interesting."*

Commenting on the B-24 that blew up on the runway [described in Chapter 5], I do remember it and saw it happen. Unless my memory is way off, it blew as it touched down. On checking later, I was told the pilot had reported bombs hung up in the bomb bay and they had let go on landing. The only part I can't pin down, Emmett, is your comment about early October 1944 (a week after your arrival). Dates are confusing. My records state that I was assigned to the 47th Wing, 17 October 1944. It was the practice then that replacement squadron COs fly a mission and visit with each Group in the Wing prior to assignment. As I recall, I flew an orientation mission with the 449th and 450th Groups while at Wing Headquarters in Manduria (no credit for flights). Then I went to San Pangrazio to fly and visit the 376th Group. I never got to the 98th Group at Lecci. Orders assigning me to the 376th Group were as of 26 October 1944. My first two sorties (four mission credits) were with the 514th Squadron on 23rd and the 29th of October prior to formal assignment. So as you see dates don't always tell of or agree with events.

Your second comment of large losses in January 1945 does not ring a bell with me; however, it did bring to mind a mission (I don't recall the date etc.), but it was a maximum effort and in the Vienna area. I was flying as Command Pilot for the 514th and we had two planes badly shot up coming off the target and losing altitude. They called me for permission to head east and leave the formation. They hoped to make it to Yugoslavia or behind the Russian lines. There was not much I could say but to wish them luck. Well, lo and behold, several weeks later, I was called to witness a group of men walking toward our squadron area all singing Russian songs and wearing Russian fur hats. To my great surprise and relief it was our two crews who went east from that mission. It was a thrill to listen to their account of those past few weeks.

Yes, I do remember getting the news of President Roosevelt's death. I was looking at the situation map in the Briefing Room and watching Capt. Avis, our Intelligence Officer, mark the Russian lines getting closer to Berlin. I will admit that the news brought tears to my eyes for a few seconds. To me, Roosevelt was a true leader and a casualty of the war. There was a certain excitement in touring with the 514th.

I guess every crewmember remembers certain flights for various reasons. Two missions come to mind for me when I go back to those days. The first was the trip to Lenz on March 31, 1945. We were lined up in a long line of squadrons leaving the I.P. The enemy was putting up "box flak." It was so black that the units ahead almost disappeared in the smoke. That was the longest two minutes I ever lived, but we arrived at the other end with no great damage.

The second mission was memorable because it was a thousand-plane raid (maximum effort). If I remember the event correctly, it was over Vienna. Whatever the cause, I'll never know, but it seemed as though several hundred planes were over the target at one time. There were units above us, below us, to the right of us, and to the left of us. I saw bombs go by me on the copilot's side and what a mess. It was one of those times that I saw an absolutely confused situation over a target. We survived that flight and all others became normal.

Returning to end on a lighter note, I also remember several fun items with a crew of deserving officers and airmen of the 514th, which you may find interesting. Capt. Warren Avis, our Intelligence Officer, was with us. He is better known now as Warren Avis of Avis Rental Car fame. We all visited the Pyramids and rode two camels. Warren borrowed an Arabian horse and rode around over the polished stones. The horse fell at full speed with Avis on it and the horse wound up on top of Avis. He was lucky. He sustained only a badly bruised leg but earned a low reputation as a horseman. In the bazaar in Cairo, I put most of my money in my watch pocket for safe keeping from pickpockets. We returned to the hotel to change uniforms and my friends pointed to my watch pocket. It had been completely cut out of my uniform. Believe it or not, it's the truth. We also bought several cases of champagne for the squadron. We had checked it over carefully to be sure it had not been tampered with. Weeks later when opened for use, we found it was filled with urine. The medics with a microscope found a hole in the top of every stopper where the contents had obviously been removed by a hypodermic needle.

Having returned to the states in 1945, I remember standing in the snow in front of the Metropolitan Theatre in Boston, accompanied by my wife, uncle, and aunt, waiting for the show to change. A young man came up to me and asked if I was Col. Taylor and I said yes. He then informed me that he was in my squadron in Italy and that it was good to see me again. What a pleasant feeling he gave me.

Finally, when we got word that we were going home, some of our more exuberant pilots gave the squadron area a buzz job. I do recall Roy Hatem being one of them. I suggested it was a little excessive when he was trying to fly under clotheslines, and I do have the pictures to prove it. Also, note page 367 in the new Liberandos book. "My meeting with you and the other crew members and members of the 514th that I had not seen in 50 years made the reunion a memorable event, especially when I got that Bear Hug from behind from my old friend, Roy Hatem."

Punk Anyone?
By Jim Snell

It was customary after returning from a mission for those of the crew who smoked to go to the waist of the plane and light up a cigarette, but only if the individual didn't have a job to do or could take a short break from it by going to the waist. Because B-17s and B-24s were the first of their kind, designed only to deliver large bomb loads and to protect themselves with turret and stationary guns, no thought was given to pressurizing the plane for the comfort of the crews. The rush of the cold outside air easily found its way into and around the waist of our plane making most attempts to light a match and then a cigarette an instant frustration. However, Jim, being the resourceful individual that he always has been, it upon the idea of using punk, a dry, decayed wood or fungi substance used as tinder and shaped like a pencil but smaller in diameter. Having excellent burning characteristics, it was easily ignited and slow to burn. Thereafter, it wasn't hard for the "punkers" to light up a cigarette and have a pleasant smoke on the way back to base.

A Case of Training and Luck
By Roy Hatem, Paul O'Steen, and Jim Snell as related to Emmett (Mac) MacKenzie

The following story occurred on March 31, 1945. Lt. Colonel Hank Taylor and Major Reno led the 514th Squadron on this mission. We were to bomb the Herman Goering Steel Works at Lenz, Austria. Our plane was the deputy lead plane. The target was heavily protected with anti-aircraft guns. The formation received one of the heaviest flak barrages that it had ever experienced. The sky was filled with "black popcorn" that appeared all around us. There was no avoiding it as we flew the bomb run on the designated heading from the IP (Initial Point of the bomb run). No turning back, no evasive action, just the target ahead was all that mattered. The Herman Goering Steel Works was partially obscured by clouds, but some of us were able to see parts of the steel works. Our plane persevered straight ahead for what seemed to be an interminable amount of time as it took hit after hit along the run. Guy toggled out our bomb load on queue from Colonel Taylor's plane after it had dropped its load and yelled over the intercom, "Bombs way!" Instinctively, Roy closed the bomb-bay doors and immediately took an oh-so-welcomed maneuver, pealing off in the direction prescribed by our box formation leader, and hopefully escaping from further flak hits sent our way by the German anti-aircraft gunners.

Although time has a way of diluting the minute-by-minute actions that occurred during our mission, some of the more memorable events never left our thoughts. Thanks to Paul's diary and Jim and Roy's recollections, it is possible to reconstruct most of the important events that took place that day. Flak had found its mark, penetrating along the entire length of the fuselage including the bomb bay. It damaged the electrical system as well as the nearby hydraulic lines. All this happened while we were making the bomb run, prior to our formation taking evasive action and heading for home. It wasn't until we were at a safe distance from the target that Paul and Jim went to the closed bomb bay to inspect and determine the extent of the plane's damage.

An exposed electrical wire had started a fire, which threatened the well being of the crew and the integrity of the plane. Jim remembered the event clearly. "I instinctively grabbed a pair of gloves from Paul and extinguished the fire. In those days, the B-24s were not equipped with fire extinguishers." Much as Jim and Paul wished that this event was the end of their problems, it was not to be. Jim remembered clearly that a hydraulic line was spewing out a fine mist of fluid throughout the bomb bay. A repair had to be made quickly to prevent the flow of hydraulic fluid from escaping from the damaged line. Paul bent the line, closed off the flow of fluid, and saved as much as possible of the precious fluid.

While Paul and Jim were in the bomb bay, another fire broke out in a small electric hydraulic pump located on the interior wall near station 5. Roy remembered this event very well. He told Bill to fly the plane and then headed for the bomb bay to see what was going on. Paul was on the catwalk and had just put out the fire with his free hand while he held onto the bomb rack with his other. All this took place at a very high altitude. Satisfied that Paul and Jim had done everything possible, Roy returned to the flight deck. Paul and Jim continued to inspect the hydraulic and electrical systems and were busy doing other makeshift repairs where possible so that the plane could return and land safely at the base.

A critical point was at hand as we drew closer to the base. Roy observed the seriousness of the hydraulic system problem as he read the accumulator pressure gauge. Instead of the normal reading between 850 and 1,000 psi, it indicated that the system had lost most of its hydraulic fluid. Roy knew that if he was lucky, there should be just enough pressure remaining in the system to permit him to lower the main and nose landing gears and to apply "one good pump" on the breaks to stop the plane after it touched down and had slowed to an absolute minimum speed before the plane ate up what was left of the runway. Roy moved the landing gear lever to the "down" position. It responded as he hoped it would. The main gear dropped down and the latches engaged, as testified by the jarring, thumping, and clanking sound of the gear as it assumed its extended position prior to landing. Both Roy and Bill did a quick bubble-window visual check on the main landing gears and determined that both main struts were fully extended and locked.

It was now Paul's turn to check on the nose wheel. He jumped down off the flight deck and headed for the nose compartment. When he got there, the nose door remained closed and the wheel in its stored position. The cause of the failure of the nose wheel door to open was the least of Paul's worries. He clicked his intercom and told Roy of the failure so Roy sent Mike down to help Paul. The design of the B-24 was such that the nose wheel doors were mechanically connected to the nose gear mechanism so that the doors opened automatically before the gear was extended and closed after the gear was retracted. Because of the crucial time factor involved, Paul elected to use brute force to make the wheel move up and over the high point of the cam system that allowed the doors to open and the wheel to drop down, but he had to have Mike's help. To dislodge the wheel, he would face the possibility of falling through the wheel-well opening as the doors responded to the movement of the wheel.

The wheel-well door opening was approximately 2 ½ feet wide by 5 feet long. First, both men straddled the outline of the closed door facing the rear of the plane. Then Mike held onto Paul's belt while Paul positioned the wheel. As planned, the doors opened and the wheel slipped noiselessly downward as a blast of cold air engulfed the compartment. But the wheel had only partially extended itself, thereby confronting the men with yet another problem to solve. Paul and Mike repositioned themselves for the final effort to extend and lock the nose gear down. Mike and Paul moved forward beyond the leading edge of the opening and secured their positions. Paul grasped his hands around the wheel well support structure in front of him while Mike extended his arms under Paul's arms and clasped his hands over Paul's chest so that he would not fall out of the plane. Then Mike helped Paul to lower himself down through the partially open area. When Paul got into position on top of the wheel, he kicked the wheel down to its extended position with both feet. Finally, after Mike pulled Paul up and out of the opening, Paul placed the pin in the lock-down position to prevent the nose wheel from folding up under pressure when making contact with the runway. Paul and Mike had given their best efforts to ensure that both crew and plane could land safely.

Notified of their success, Roy lined up the plane with the runway, lowered the wing flaps, reduced the speed to a minimum, and began his letdown, glide-pattern heading toward the near end of the runway in preparation for landing. Roy remembers landing the plane on that very eventful day as he conjured up fifty years of flying memories. "Only one problem remained, having landed. How could I stop the plane before running out of runway? The hydraulic gauges indicated only a slight flutter of hydraulic pressure. Much of the fluid was gone. One good pump and that was all that I was going to get out of the breaking system to help stop the plane. Hopefully, our luck would hold out. Looking for a way to slow down the plane, I called Lou and asked if our parachutes could be secured to the waist gun mounts and be opened as we landed thus assisting in slowing down the plane." Lou, Byron, and I were unable to carry out this plan as the gun mounts or other stationary fixtures were not compatible for hooking up the parachutes' outer packaging. Ultimately, we had to trust to luck.

"After we landed and were approaching the far end of the runway, I applied the brakes cautiously slowing the plane down just enough to turn onto the last taxi strip. Hydraulic pressure was almost zero. I braked and turned onto the left wheel. The plane gradually rotated to a stop. The hardstand I turned into and parked on was not ours and the crew chief raised hell about it. But when I read him off and told him the plane had no brakes and that I had turned off on the first available hard stand to clear the taxi strip for other planes, not to mention the possible danger of our plane colliding with other planes ahead of us, he quieted down. Later our plane was towed to its proper hardstand and its ground crew began counting the holes in it. A count of 125 holes was recorded. It was at this point the crew chief said, 'Why did you have to bring this sieve back? Why didn't you just ditch it somewhere in the Adriatic Sea? Now we are going to have to work a hell-of-a-lot of hours to get it back in shape to fly again.' With no thought of the fact that this B-24 had brought our crew home safely, this display of ingratitude voiced by the crew chief rankled the feelings of all the crewmembers. Once again, we were 'Fortune's Favorites' and had made it through another mission."

A Case of Extra Sensory Perception

"I don't remember on what mission the following event took place, but I vividly remember the event itself. We had just completed the bomb run and were about to take the predetermined evasive action. We were to "peel off" to the right and lose altitude quickly. The area we were to enter was clear of flak. What better way to go? Up and ahead the sky was filled with the black smoke emanating from the explosion of antiaircraft shells. Then suddenly without knowing why, I knew I had to pull up and head straight into the smoke filled sky." We flew through the area with no new flak explosions taking place, while down below us and to the right, the sky had become dense blanket of black smoke. I had made the right decision for saving crew and plane."

The Lenz Mission: Good Friday
By Mike Ozkcus

I remember Lenz, Austria, not because we bombed it on Good Friday, but because of the beating it gave us. Lenz was an industrial city right on the Danube. It had the Herman Goering Tank Works, the Herman Goering Steel Works, etc. We took a severe beating at this target. Everybody was hit hard. The ground crew chief of our plane told me we had come home with over a hundred and fifty holes in our plane. Maybe it was on this flight that our front landing gear would not come down because of a piece of flak that had dented it. To get it down, O'Steen lay on his back with his feet and legs extended over the open wheel well while I had my arms under his armpits and my hands clasped over his chest. He must have trusted me, but we had no choice. He kept kicking the gear with his feet and legs until the land gear dropped down so that he could lock it with a pin.

It was on this flight that O'Steen and some of the crewmembers had to put out a fire in the bomb bay. The flak guns came close this time, but they didn't get us. At another time, there were bombs hung up on their hangers in the bomb bay. They were only partially released and could not be re-hung in their original position. With the bomb bay doors open and nothing but 23,000 feet of air space between them and the earth, Guy and Paul kicked them out.

After having flown on Good Friday to Lenz, which had all but destroyed us. I also had flown on the next day, which I guess is Holy Saturday. On Easter Sunday, I was back in the briefing room. Friday's Lenz sortie was behind us and we were back to that team that was ready for the next game and the next "Go!" pep talk. After the usual call for "Attention!" and the "Be-seated" invitation, we went back to chatting and laughing. Then the cloth covering the target was dropped. It was Lenz again. Some of us at this briefing had just returned from Lenz less than 36 hours earlier. We just sat there in silence. Fate with its fickle finger was screwing us again. As the briefing began, we just sat there staring at the map. Nobody was paying attention to the briefing officer. We had heard it all before. Each man had his own thoughts. We just stared into space. We would get into our planes, hit Lenz and take what Lenz had waiting for us. It was all out of our hands.

Right after the briefing, for the first time ever, the chaplain showed up. I remember his words exactly. "I had hoped that I would see you all in church this morning. Since you could not come to me, I have come to you. Let us pray." While he was praying, someone stepped up to the briefing officer and said something to him. When the prayer was finished, the briefing officer said, "Lenz is overcast and is aborted. You will proceed to your secondary target." At that moment we all knew that there was a God. Never had so few men raised such a loud and spontaneous cheer.

Reminisces
By Emmett (Mac) MacKenzie

The Great Celebration: The Birth of Major Reno's Son

The parties were just starting to get lively in both the Officer's Club and the Enlisted Men's Club. Word had just been received that day that Major Reno was the father of a newborn son. To celebrate the event, the Major threw a party for all squadron personnel. Wine, whisky, vodka, and cognac flowed freely in both the clubs. Until this time, I believe that I had never taken a drink of liquor, since I was such a "good Baptist." But temptation got the better of me. Encouraged by my fellow ground crewmember, he and I went to the Enlisted Men's club. On entering the place, we could see liquor being poured in an unending stream of merriment. Everyone was talking and laughing—sometimes yelling at each other. A sense of well being prevailed with only a passing thought of why we were gathered together here as individuals, crews, or squadron members on this spot of land, a former olive grove. It was as if there was no war being fought.

My friend and I found a space at the bar and began ordering one drink after another. Shortly thereafter, I was ordering multiple mixed drinks. But my drinking ended all too quickly. All revelry, merriment, and comradeship ceased. The time and events were completely masked out by unconsciousness. I never saw my fellow celebrant again. Someone at the club got the word out to my crew to come and get me. It was Mike to the rescue. He was the Officer of the Day, thank God. He made sure that I got back to the tent. I woke up some time after midnight and was sick beyond belief. The next twelve hours were undoubtedly the most miserable hours I ever spent in my life, to say nothing of the problems I inflicted on my caring fellow tent dwellers. With the coming of morning, I thought I would not make it through the day. But as time passed, my excruciating headache subsided and my life returned to normal. Much to their credit, the guys never once mentioned the incident to me, neither did Mike. Fortunately for all concerned, our crew was not listed to fly that day. However, I shall never forget that celebration or the price that I paid for it. I never went back to the club again.

R & R on the Resort Island of Capri

The Island of Capri lies approximately 30 miles south and slightly east of Naples. A mountain range runs north to south through the island, dividing it into two major saddle-shaped areas. Since prehistoric times, the island had been inhabited and controlled since 600 BCE first by the Greek colonists, then by the city-state of Naples, and finally by the Romans. The island served then, as it does today, as the home of local fishermen and their families. They lived a quiet life making a living by catching and selling the fish they caught to the population of Naples and the surrounding areas. It was during this period that Naples couldn't resist the appeal of the resort potential of the island and absorbed the Isle of Capri into her city-state.

The book, *Capri*, has this to add about the history of the island: "In 29 A.D., Ottaviano, not yet Augustus, sailed towards Naples and was attracted by the soaring cliffs and the gigantic peaks of the Faraglion. He landed at Capri and was so delighted by its quiet beauty that he did not hesitate to withdraw the island from Naples's grasp and make it part of the growing principality. After Augustus's death in 14 A.D.,

Tiberius followed Augustus as ruler of the Roman Empire and lived on the island, conducting all the affairs of state and business from Capri. He also built twelve villas, the same number as the twelve divinities of Olympus"

After the decline and fall of the Roman Empire, the island once again returned to the quiet way of life it had known prior to its discovery by Augustus. In this setting, and over a period of time, churches and monasteries were built to serve the religious needs of the people of the villages. Obviously, the island was a favorite spot for R & R before and after WWI; but it was during the ascendancy of Mussolini, the self proclaimed leader of all Italians, that he built a palace on Ana Capri during the early 1930's. The island once more had regained the prominence and the attention of the German-Italian Military Axis. During 1943, the allies captured Sicily and began the long quest to set the whole of Italy (including the Isle of Capri) free from Fascist and Nazi domination.

The town of Ana Capri lay to the south, and the town of Capri lay to the east side of an outcropping mountain range that separated the two towns. Remember and visualize, if you will, the sights and sounds of 50 years ago. The only entrance to the island was guarded by a sea wall and a lighthouse centrally located near the edge of what seemed to be a restrictive sea passageway on the east side of the island. Behind the wall was the Marina Grande, where all the sea commerce and tourist trade flowed in and out of the harbor. The tracks of the incline railroad, the Funicular, traced out a path up the side of a steep cliff some one hundred feet or more above the harbor. It probably was the crew's first ride on an inclined rail system. "At the top, one could look out over the whole of the Marina Grande from the terrace known as the Belvedere or the "little Balcony." It is situated in the open space at the terminus of the funicular railway surrounded by colonnades."

The centerpiece and gathering place for the village of Capri was the Piazza Umberto. This town square was surrounded by small shops and sidewalk cafes, which served both food and drink. At one end of the square was the church of Santo Stefano, modeled after the Baroque style of architecture. The church had been rebuilt several times on the site of an Ancient Cathedral. Leading from the church and the shops across from it, separated by a narrow passageway, was a set of staircases fanning out into the square itself. The setting of the town square remains essentially unchanged today.

After 51 years it is very difficult to pin down the exact date that our turn came to get away from the war. The probable time frame was during the first two weeks of March 1945. It was then that the orders were cut and we left on a B-24 shuttle plane from San Pangrazio to Naples, a distance of approximately 200 miles (322 km). Within an hour and a half, we were lugging our B-2 clothing bags off the plane and heading for the Naples harbor where the ferry was waiting to take service personnel to Capri harbor. The ferry churned away from the dock and headed southwest for 20 miles. It wasn't long before we were disembarking at the Isle of Capri. My thoughts were "What a great place this is, and what a good time we're going to have." It was unreal! I hardly could comprehend the fact that we had "toughed out" the war that now seemed so far away; and that we had finally made it to this paradise in the Mediterranean.

But I believe the war had left our crew with a void that could not be filled. Andy would never see Capri with us or participate in our experiences here. His absence would continue to be felt long after his departure.

The officers were assigned quarters at the Grand Marina Hotel near the harbor, and the enlisted men were assigned quarters at the El Morgano Hotel, overlooking the entire harbor. It was elegant compared to the officer's hotel. To access our quarters, the enlisted men took the Funicular and disembarked on to the Belvedere located near the edge of the Piazzetta.

We were guided to the hotel where we were assigned to rooms. What a luxurious feeling it was to have indoor plumbing, a shower stall, comfortable beds, tile floors, and clean glass windows to look out. It was a far cry from the dirt-ridden floor and the dusty windowless tent that we had called home for six months. On the first morning of our stay, we arose at 7:30, showered, put on our olive drab dress uniforms and headed to the large spacious veranda. It was surrounded by palm trees and bougainvillea-covered colonnades that overlooked the Marina below. This had to be Heaven on earth! What a beautiful sight to behold, and here we were right in the middle of it soaking up all the sights, sounds, and smells of a newly discovered existence. We selected the breakfast of our choice and were served at tables on a very large veranda, which was attached to the prestigious hotel Morgano, from which we could overlook the harbor, and toward Naples on the mainland.

I remember that the enlisted men decided to go down to the Marina and hire a local guide to row us out the Grotto Azzurra, "the Blue Grotto," a famous cave located on the northwest corner of the island. The entry to the cave was a shallow opening that existed only when the tide was low. Otherwise the water sealed it off. The thought of being trapped in the cave did give rise to the concern for our safety. However, the venture was interesting as the water in the cave was a pure translucent light bluish color caused by the refraction of the sunlight through the water outside of the cave. Jim remembers a couple of Italian rowing guides discussing their experiences in the Italian Army and wondered if they harbored any grievances against Americans. After a short period of time we exited the cave and were on our way back to the hotel for lunch.

Both the officers and the enlisted men had their own agenda, but we did find time to make several outings and explorations together. One of these was to go down to the Marina and have a real Italian spaghetti-and-meatball dinner replete with beer or soft drink. The food was some of the best we had eaten in a long time. On another occasion, we went on a tour of one of Tiberius's villas, Jovis.

According to the book, *Capri*, "The villa crowns the eastern headland of the island where Jupiter and his earthly pontiff Tiberius could surround themselves with threatening and brilliant splendor. Villa Jovis the largest and best conserved of the island's imperial villas unites historical interest and the singular beauty of the site. Near the entrance to the excavations is the so-called 'Tiberius Jump,' a frightening rocky precipice 183 feet (297 meters) above the sea, from where, according to tradition, Tiberius forced his political adversaries to leap." [4] As a crew, we were aware of the villa's significance but were not overly impressed by our surroundings, except for the baths, winery, and the jumping off point. Otherwise, we viewed it as just a sun-drenched, windswept, dusty, and deteriorating remnant of a once proud and prestigious historical site.

On another occasion, one of our officers heard about a "black market" restaurant tucked away on a hillside above the town, which specialized in fried eggs and bacon served with fried potatoes, all for one very special price. All the crewmembers thought it was a good idea and agreed to go on this little adventure. It was Friday evening, and the dusk of the day was settling rapidly on the island. But before we could leave the Piazzetta, we had to wait for Mike to go to confession. By the time we got under way, it had become pitch black with no moon to guide our way. We stumbled up a rocky path until we saw a small one-story building separated from the night by a small overhanging light fixture with a dimly lit bulb which faintly illuminating the structure. All agreed that the food was good. What else would one expect? After all, the place was "off limits" to military personnel.

On a typical evening on the Piazzetta, with service personnel coming and going, boisterous talk and laughter filled the air. The tables around the outdoor cafes were crowded with guys eating and drinking beer. This was the setting in which Bill, Byron, Paul, Jim, and other members of our crew found themselves. On this occasion, Bill asked Paul to lend him a set of Paul's uniforms before going to the town center. The crewmembers bought their beers and found an empty table to sit around. At some point during the evening, Bill stood up and told those present to hang onto his chair as he was going over to the bar to get another beer. Only a short time had elapsed when a big red headed Staff Sergeant spotted the empty chair, sat down, and claimed it for his use. An admonition was issued against occupying the chair but he paid no heed. The crewmembers smiled inwardly as they knew those present in the Piazzetta were in for an exciting time when Bill returned, but the Sergeant had been warned, hadn't he? On returning to the table, Bill walked over to Sergeant and told him that he wanted his chair back. The Sergeant told Bill no one was sitting in the chair when he took it and said that it was his now. The

Sergeant's reply had the effect of waving a red flag in front of a bull. A fight immediately ensued and the Sergeant ended up with a black eye, less one chair. The briefly interrupted merriment continued in full swing as if nothing had happened. Now the reader should understand why Bill went by the name "Wild Bill Hickok."

As a postscript, Bill encountered the Staff Sergeant on our return trip back to Naples; only this time Bill was dressed in his officer's uniform. The thoughts of the Sergeant were never verbally expressed.

A Young Boy's Plea

On the last night before our departure for the mainland, I had gone to the Piazzetta and was sitting alone at a table. It was a relatively quiet night in the town square and only a small number of people were present. As I sat there contemplating the end of my brief stay on Capri, a young boy approached me and asked me in broken English, "Hey, Joe! Wanna buy a souvenir?" I told him that I had enough stuff to take back with me already, but as we continued to talk, I discovered his real motive. "I wanna go to America. Will you take me with you?" I explained to him that I was not going back to America but was returning to our base with my crew to continue flying. "How about after you win the war?" he asked. I had never contemplated being asked such a soul-searching question and was unable to give him the answer he was seeking. He departed in sadness. I remained seated there, feeling the anguish of not being able to fulfill his desire for a new and better life. I have always wondered what happened to him in his quest for a new life in America the Beautiful.

Naples and Pompeii

On returning to Naples, our crew discovered that we had unintentionally missed the last flight for the week, which would have gotten our crew back to the 514th Squadron as scheduled. The answer to the question, "What to do?" was not long in coming. We would wait another week for the next flight and see the sights of Naples and the surrounding area. It was not a far stretch of the imagination by the crew to assume that Roy had planned it that way.

The next day, singularly or in small groups, we walked the beaches or visited the Naples Museum. We walked the main thoroughfares, venturing ever so carefully into the entrance to a forbidden ghetto. We climbed up the narrow and roughly cut worn stone stairways, all the while looking up at people leaning out their windows or standing on their balconies jabbering back and forth with each other. Later we observed the street hawkers noisily trying to get GIs to buy their wares. All GIs were fair game! The street scene was that of a large, open, circular town square boasting stone park benches, palm trees, and large inlayed stone walking areas. That evening, the square was a noisy, bustling, laughing, cheerful tide of humanity. Having had enough of the local scene, the other crewmembers returned to the base except for me.

After walking the central piazza with the other enlisted men, I decided to take in the local performance of Othello at the San Carlos Opera House. The building and its Marquee were nondescript. The exterior of the building was only lit sparsely with a number of white lights. Inside, the motif was that of the early '30s movie in the states but probably much more ornate. When the opera *Othello* began, I was struck by the staging. The props and lighting were outstanding. It was as if you were in some US big city theater. The singers were well rehearsed but I just couldn't stay wake near the end. The audience was given a program written in English describing the plot in limited detail. It was hard to read in the dark. Perhaps if I had understood the plot better, it would have made a difference in my alertness. However, as you might have guessed by now, all the dialogue and lyrics was spoken and sung in Italian. At the end of the play the audience clapped with appreciation and there were many cries of "Bravo! Bravo! Bravo!" In retrospect, it was an interesting venture and good entertainment for a mere 50 Lira, an Italian monetary script and used by the Allies, which included the Italians at the time.

Pompeii, Italy

Near the end of our stay at the Naples air base, I heard Pompeii was a short distance away, only 15 or 20 miles to the ruins by train. Since I could not persuade any of the other enlisted men to go with me, I decided to go there along. (I learned since that some of the officers went there the same day.) At its pinnacle, Pompeii had become a renowned cultural center. It was noted for its agricultural and wool products, commerce, government buildings, industry, good living, and Greek and Roman shrines.

The book, *Capri*, states, "Pompeii had been founded by the aboriginal Oscan people and thereafter conquered and occupied by Greeks, Etruscans (whose language has been traced back to the Albanians), and by a belligerent Italic race called the Samnites who greatly expanded it. About 80 B.C., Rome had made it a colony, adding to its prosperity. This evolving occupation took place over a period of many centuries prior to Pompeii's ultimate destruction. In the year 62 A.D., the people had survived the first recorded devastating volcanic eruption of Mt. Versifies and had rebuilt their city. However seventeen years later, A.D. 79, the people witnessed and were consumed by the awesome and destructive power of Mt. Vesuvius. "Accumulating at the rate of 15 centimeters (6 inches) per hour for 11 hours, Pompeii and it people were buried under 2.7 meters (9 feet) of ash and pumice fallout as buildings and roofs caved in under the tremendous weight of debris spewed out during the second eruption. Death claimed its victims by smothering them in ash and killing them with sulfurous gases release by the eruption." Much of the population was entombed in layers of volcanic dust and hot ash forming a sarcophagus around their bodies, preserving them for posterity. Pompeii was not to be rediscovered until excavation began in 1709.

The excavation of Pompeii remains a slow and tedious ongoing process. I understand that now much of the area where I walked in 1945 has been closed off because of the weakened and dangerous condition of some of the ancient buildings. This visit made a lasting impression on me—the broad parkway that led to their municipal, justice, and senate buildings; the narrow cobblestone streets, deeply etched by the wheels of chariots of that period of time; the stepping stones raised above the street so that the inhabitants would not get their feet wet when crossing the street; the storefronts selling wines, breads and much more; the temples dedicated to their special gods; the bath houses open to all the city dwellers; and finally the residences of the well-to-do citizens. I saw the petrified body of a male slave, identified as such by his belt. He was exhibited lying in the courtyard outside a public bathhouse. That ashen piece of humanity gave me insight into the great natural catastrophe, which had occurred centuries ago.

I returned to Naples by train late in the afternoon, absorbing all that I had seen and heard. Since it was the rush hour for service personnel and local people returning to Naples, they filled the seats of the open-windowed passenger coaches and then spilled out into the aisles, the entryways, and the coach entry steps while the less fortunate locals clung to any exterior part of the coach that offered a hand and toe hold.

The First and Last Home Improvement Project

Always looking for a way to improve our lives in Tent City, Paul, Jim and maybe Byron had been told about the crates in which fragmentary bombs had been stored in the armament depot. One day, while they were rummaging around the squadron's armament storage facility, they saw many the empty creates lying around. It was at that moment that the idea for the next home improvement project began to evolve. They came back to the tent and told Lou and me what they had seen. "You know," said Jim, "We could really put those crates to good use. First, we should make sure that the dirt floor surface is flat and smooth. Then if we carefully take the crates apart and made a floor frame, we can lay and nail down strips making a good wooden floor in our tent. Think about it! We could be walking around in our stocking feet on a clean and smooth wooden floor, not having to worry about dust and dirt." With that, we all agreed to help put down the first wooden floor in the enlisted men's area. What a grand idea! The crates were simple in structure-perhaps three feet long with approximately one foot square pieces of wood at each end. The ends were connected on each of their sides with four strips of lath approximately an inch and a half wide and an inch thick, 12 pieces in all for each crate. Like the good scavengers that we were, the five of us lugged many crates from the armament section back to our tent area. Working with a total of 144 square feet in mind, it probably took at least 108 crates to get enough wood to cover the area, not to mention the supporting framework on which the strips had to be nailed down with meticulous care. Several days were to elapse before the floor was in place. We celebrated by inviting Guy, Bill, Mike, and Roy over to see our handiwork. It was not an infrequent occurrence to have them in our tent talking or playing cards. Our morale was high and we felt good.

The Very Special and Memorable Day: The Beginning of the End

We had just begun to appreciate our newly laid tent floor and were satisfied with the efforts of our labors, when we got orders from squadron headquarters. The 376th Heavy Bomber Group was to be deactivated and our crew was to move to Foggia, Italy. The word came to us on the same day that President Roosevelt died, April 12, 1945. I will always remember that day as one of depression and rejection. We all wanted to go home with the 376th Bomb Group but, with the exception of Mike, no member of the crew had achieved 50 missions, the magic number that qualified a man to return home. The missions flown by members of the crew varied between 31 and 50 missions per man for such reasons as sickness, mental fatigue, and essential new-crew-member-familiarization missions. The play-out of events was to be determined by one of two options available to the crew. Either we could return to the states and train on B-29s if the crew remained intact, or we had to move up to Foggia and hopefully finish out our 50 missions there. The former option had to be satisfied in order to go stateside.

It was at this point that the officers took a straw vote among themselves to decide whether we remained in Italy or went home. Mike, having finished his 50 missions, was eligible to return to the states. For this reason, he would not agree to any more tours of duty, especially if it meant going to the Pacific Theatre. Therefore, the depleted crew was left with the remaining option. We all understood Mike's rationale for not staying with the crew. He had done what was required of him and he wanted to go home.

Roy came over to our tent and told us that we would be staying in Italy and moving up to Foggia, and to start packing up our gear. Jim remembers that after Roy left our tent, Paul could not contain his frustration. He was mad and disappointed as we all were. But Paul had to vent his anger out on something so he took a "two by four" and hammered away on the stovepipe and the 50-gallon barrel stove that had served us well over a period of six months. The battering of the pipe and the stove didn't really matter that much. And Paul had relieved his frustration, at least temporarily. We departed the 514th Squadron and the 376th HBG forever, and were on our way to Foggia, Italy two days later on April 14th.

Crew 313 participated in the following missions 376th Bomb Group. Mission No. 421, March 1, 1945

Mission status:

- Target: Vienna, Austria; Moosbierbaum Oil Refinery
- Flight time: 7:25 hours
- Target distance: Approx. 570 miles (924 km)
- Crew points: 2 sorties, 1 mission

Aircraft statistics:

- Aircraft at takeoff: 26
- Aircraft over target: 24

- Aircraft returning to base: 26
- Aircraft diverted or forced to land: 0
- Aircraft damaged: 0

Mission summary:

- Bomb load: 130 500-lb bombs
- Bombing results: No entry
- No navigational/bombing radar: No visual observation due to weather
- Fighter escort: 40 P-51s
- Enemy aircraft: 1 German Me 263 (jet engine fighter), S.E. 6
- Mission commentary: This was the first mission for our New C.O. Col. Warren.

376th Bomb Group, Mission No. 434, March 22, 1945

Mission status:

- Target: Vienna, Austria; Ordinance Depot (S.E.)
- Flight time: 7:10 hours
- Target distance: Approx. 482 miles (777 km)
- Crew points: 2 sorties, 1 mission

Flight leaders:

- A Flight: Lt, Col. George, Lt. Hill (513th Squadron)
- B Flight: Lt. Hatem (514th Squadron)

- C Flight: Lt. Witkin (515th Squadron), Lt., Summers (515th Squadron)

Aircraft statistics:

- Aircraft at takeoff: 40
- Aircraft over target: 35
- Aircraft returning to base: 39
- Aircraft diverted or forced to land: 1

Mission summary:

- Bomb load: No Entry by 514th Squadron
- Bombing results: No Entry by 514th Squadron
- Anti-aircraft fire: No entry
- Mission's commentary: It was almost a perfect bombing run. The 514th Squadron placed 90% of their bombs within 600 feet of the bull's-eye. Guy had one of his best days as a bombardier.

> **Paul's diary:** Today our target was Vienna, Austria. We bombed the main railroad marshalling yard and ordinance depot. The target was clear and we practically wiped it out. Flak was the worst we have ever gotten. A lot of wires were shot out, and the nose gear was damaged. I put the wires together, giving us power to our superchargers and over the field. I had to kick the nose gear down. All of our planes got back. It was my seventeenth sortie, twenty-ninth mission. Hope we never bomb that place visually again.

> **Author's comment:** Based on Paul's diary entry, the anti-aircraft must have been heavy, moderate, and accurate.

376th Bomb Group, Mission No. 440, March 31, 1945

Mission status:

- Target: Lenz, Austria; Herman Goering Steel Works
- Flight time: 8:20 hours
- Target distance: Approx. 520 miles (838km)
- Crew points: 2 sorties, 1 mission

Flight leaders:

- A Flight: Lt. Col. Taylor (514th Squadron)
- B Flight: Lt. Norris (513th Squadron)
- C Flight: Lt. Feak (512th Squadron)
- D Flight: Lt. Kock (515th Squadron)

Aircraft statistics: No entry

Mission summary:

- Bombing results: All four squadrons flew that day. The mission was lead by Col. Henry Taylor of the 514th Squadron. The group bombed through clouds. Photos showed several direct hits on the target.
- Mission Commentary: Unknown to our Crew, this was to be its last mission with the 514th Squadron. The Liberandos Group 376 was ordered to disband after April 12, 1945.

Paul's diary: Today we bombed the main railroad marshalling yard at Lenz, Austria. It is a toss up whether this target or Vienna is the worst. I don't believe they wasted a shot today. Every one of them hit somebody. They shot out our hydraulic system and I had to take my flak suit off over the target so that I could work on it. I was busy in the bomb bay all the way home. A fire started from a hot wire and Jim Snell grabbed it with his glove and put it out. If hydraulic fluid were highly flammable, we wouldn't be here today.

Two of our ships were so badly shot up, they headed for the Russian lines. The lead ship had an engine shot out, and the bombardier on one of the other ships was killed instantly with piece of flak. Back over the base, I cranked the main gear down by hand, and kicked the nose wheel out. We had no brakes and the plane ran off the end of the runway before we stopped. Thank God no one got hurt. This was my eighteenth sortie and thirty-first mission.

Author's comment: Note Paul's dedication to his job. This was to be Paul's last entry in his diary. He and the other crewmembers probably were experiencing a psychological let down. Unquestionably, he had become very fatigued and lost interest in keeping a further record of his sorties/missions with commentary.

The crew owes Paul a debt of gratitude for keeping a record of his and our sorties and missions for as long as he did. No one else had the foresight and interest to record their thoughts of the events that were taking place.

13

Foggia, Italy: April to May 1945

Scavenging GI Issue and the Move to Foggia, Italy
By Emmett (Mac) MacKenzie

On first thought, one would think that we as a crew would have had enough to pack into our B-2 Duffle Bags as we prepared to leave the 514th, but there were other considerations. Here were all these lucky crews that were about to ship out to the states and who were limited as to what they could take aboard ship with them when they left for the US Naval Base at Taranto, Italy, some 50 miles or so to our base. Never let it be said that aircrews and ground crews alike were not a bunch of pack rats. There were new and used government-issued binoculars, 45cal. pistols, watches, clothing, etc. So members of our crew negotiated and rapidly acquired selected items that they thought could be used at the new base. We had much more luggage at the time of our departure than when we arrived at the 514th Bomb Squadron, some seven months before—a lifetime before.

On April 14, we departed for Foggia, the headquarters of the 15th Air Force and the 461 Heavy Bomb Group. Mike thought he remembered all of us departing the 514th on a C-47. He said it was so heavily laden with baggage, our crew, and other military materials that either the plane couldn't carry the load or it developed engine problems and had to land at another air base a short distance away. In any event, we traveled the remainder of the distance in a big old lumbering Army truck. My recollection was that our crew was issued an Army truck to move to Foggia. All I remember was that Roy, Bill, and Guy rode in the cab while the enlisted men sat on bench seats attached to the interior sides of the truck bed.

It was my impression that Mike had stayed behind and would depart with the 376th via Taranto or fly home on another B-24. The ride in the truck reminded me of our first trip in Italy—hot and dirty. We rode on a dusty dirt road from San Pangrazio passing through Mesagne, San Vito Normanni, Ostuni, Fasano, and then drove along the beach road bordering the Adriatic Sea to Bari, Molfetta, Barietta, and finally arrived at Foggia. Sometime after passing through Ostuni, we entered a desolate area comprised of rolling hills, a few trees, and a creek running through the hills. It was here that we stopped, jumped out of the truck, undressed down to our skivvies, and jumped into a two or three foot deep smooth rock-bottomed pool of water carved out by the creek. The water was enjoyable and relaxing. Then we got dressed and ate our K-Ration lunch and took off again.

It was here that I realized that, once again, we were short one more crewmember: Mike. There was to be no more Mike-jokes and laughter to lighten our lives. He was gone from our midst, as was Andy. The circle of comradeship was broken forever.

We were back on the road within an hour and a half, and soon thereafter, we reached the shores of the Adriatic at the little town of Monopoli. We continued along the shore road until we reached Barletta stopping about the middle of the afternoon. We headed for the beach and goofed around for a short time watching the waves roll in toward shore. It was too cool for swimming at that time of the year. Yet we all remembered what was beyond the eastern horizon of the sea because we had flown over Yugoslavia, that war torn land, many times. From our current location, it was less than 30 miles (48 km) inland to Foggia. In all, we had traveled over 150 miles (240 km) since early morning.

Having arrived and checked in at the 461st Group Headquarters, it was clear that they were not prepared to receive us with accommodations resembling those with which we left a few short hours earlier. Instead, we were led to a large area surrounded by a four-foot brick fence. In the center was a large brick and tiled roof building. This was to be our residence. It was complete with a vaulted wooden-beamed ceiling. Brick wainscoted walls rose up to about seven feet above the floor. Above the wainscoting, the walls were white washed. The floors were also brick strewn with straw. Low rising wall partitions divided off the large open space. At the one end of the building a partitioned area was set aside where army cots had been placed for our crew. Could we ask for anything better than this large whitewashed horse barn to rest our weary bones? Undoubtedly, the property had once belonged to a well-to-do landowner.

After stowing our gear, the enlisted men and the officers were shown to their respective shower buildings and mess halls located in another area of the base. It was a great feeling to be clean once again. We put on clean uniforms and headed for the mess hall. Returning to the barn, it wasn't long before night and sleep overtook our weary bodies and we drifted off into unconsciousness. The horse barn was to serve as the crew's sleeping quarter for the remainder of our stay in Italy.

The next morning as we exited the barn, we were greeted by shouts and laughter. A bunch of young men were playing soccer in the courtyard. They were happy, boisterous, and alive with energy. I had never heard of or ever seen for that matter anyone playing this game before. It was quite a sight to behold watching them controlling, kicking, and bouncing the ball off there heads as they laughed and drove for the opposite team's goal posts.

Not long after we had left the 514th Squadron, Roy and Bill deemed a return trip necessary. Of course Paul and maybe some other crewmembers may have been present as they returned to the 514th Squadron and flew up and over the road leading to the 514th Squadron Headquarters "Main Street" and did one last and very low level buzz job. After all, the street did need a good clean sweep. (We have photos verifying this fact. That's probably another reason why Col. Henry Taylor remembers Roy so well.)

Back to our Prime Directive:
The Destruction of German War Capabilities in Northern Italy
As told to Emmett (Mac) MacKenzie by Jim Snell

We flew four more missions all over northern Italy. Little did we know that the war was actually winding down very rapidly in Southern Europe. To our crew, it was just one mission after another dropping 500 pounders on the fleeing enemy during the last two weeks of April. We flew two back-to-back missions because of the grievous error made on the first bombing mission. The area in question was the Bolzano-Bozen, some 87 miles (141km) from the city of Verona in Northern Italy. The Germans were retreating as fast as possible through Bolzano-Bozen heading toward Innsbruck, Austria 73 miles (118 km) away via the Brenner Pass located on the border of Italy. The mission of the 461st was to cut off the German escape route by bombing ahead (north) of the German Troops. In hot pursuit were American and British troops.

The two opposing armies were so close together that the Allied Command decided to establish a line of demarcation between them. The Allies would light smudge pots all along the line giving off black smoke that made it easier for the Air Force to find its target. However, two critical factors were not anticipated: The black smoke from the smudge pots was difficult to see from the air and, because of air currents, the smoke drifted southward toward the allied troops. As a result, the Air Force including the 461st bombed the area south of the smoke line. The casualties to the Allies were considerable. Almost before we had returned to base after the mission, word was received by the 461st that we had bombed our own troops. The same mission was repeated again the next day. This time, white smoke was used, the smoke did not drift southward, and the mission came off successfully—but what a price in human life was paid to bring off that one mission!

Vincent van Gogh's Painted Fields of Poppies

The weather was moderating. It was now late in April and spring was returning to Italy. Prior to one of our last missions, I beheld an amazing sight. As our plane picked up speed and was rolling down the runway, I looked out the open left waist window and saw a hillside painted in brilliant red and yellow Italian poppies. But when we were airborne and had circled the base, the red poppies disappeared and all that was left were fields of yellow poppies. It was my first experience and lesson concerning the effect of the sun's absorption spectrum. Only the color red was absorbed while the color yellow was reflected back to earth. By definition, "red was the one color of the collection of wavelengths missing from a continuous distribution of wave lengths caused by the absorption of certain wave lengths by the atoms or molecules in a gas." Nevertheless, it was a sight that I will never forget.

The Month of May: The Days of Feasting

As soon as it was known that the war was over and the Germans had surrendered, one vital logistical problem presented itself to the 15th Air Force. What was to be done about the tons on tons of food supplies that were stored in warehouses in and around Foggia? Supplies couldn't be left to spoil or to be given to the local population after the departure from Italy. This was a very important command decision that had to be made quickly. The decision was made, orders were issued, the appropriate course of action was implemented, and it was left to wise procurement officers of each group to carry out the orders. Why of course: "Feed the airmen like they had never been fed before during their three-year stay in Italy." Problem solved. Early in May, the mess hall's menu changed dramatically. Breakfast featured ham, bacon and eggs and biscuits and gravy. While assigned to the 376th, we were lucky to have eggs once a month, but now the sky was the limit. A menu of steak, ham, fish, or chicken was not unusual for lunch or supper along with all the appropriate condiments associated with each main course. We feasted royally the last month of our stay in Italy. But since those days, I have often mused as to why the above menus could not have been spread a little more evenly over the period of our stay in Italy.

Lest the reader gets the wrong idea about our tour of duty in Italy, it should be noted that practice missions were part of our itinerary each month regardless of the group to which we were assigned. While assigned to the 376th HB Group, it was not abnormal to fly two or three of these missions to improve our marksmanship or to check out the new navigational equipment, the Mickey Radar system, for example. On other occasions, the flights might entail flying to a supply depot to pick up what ever was needed by the squadron, i.e. food or plane parts. High on the priority list were food and liquor supplies for the squadron mess hall and the Officer and Enlisted Men's clubs.

Excitement Texas Style

It was now early in June. Our crew only had been assigned to the 461st Bomb Group since April 17th. The war in Europe would be over on June 8th and the 461st Group itself was now getting ready to pull up stakes and head back to the states. In preparation for the impending move, an order was issued to get rid of all the 50-gallon fuel cans in the squadron. This was accomplished in a short time by blowing them up. Bill and another officer mused over the possibility as to how to use this incident to create a little more excitement. Coincidentally there was a group of Texans who kept to themselves and didn't mix with the rest of the officers in the encampment. So Bill and his friend decided to liven things up a little bit. Having made the decision, the next question was how to accomplish the mission. Then out of the blue, an idea and a plan evolved and became crystal clear to them. Scrounging around, they were able to find and collect 50cal. machine gun bullets in addition to 37mm cannon shells. Like shadows in the night, Bill and his friend snuck up to a barrel containing combustible waste that was near the Texan encampment. They tossed in the ammunition, lit the waste material, and withdrew to a hiding place to watch their labor bear fruit.

It wasn't long in coming. The shells quickly heated up to a temperature sufficient to cause the ammunition to begin exploding. Bullets began whizzing around every which way. The Texans taken by surprise likewise began to flee the area in all directions, fortunately without injury. Bill and his friend lay in the grass rolling around in laughter, hardly being able to keep their hiding place a secret. "What a great send off for the Texans!" Bill and his friend thought.

G.I. Humor at Its Worst: Two Outhouse Stories
By Michael Oczkus

In the middle of April 1945, the war was winding down and we were running out of targets. As a result, the decision was made to disband the 376HBGroup. An order was issued that nothing was going to be left behind or left standing. So the demolition crews started to dynamite all the structures, etc. In the evening, it was party, party, party. In the daytime it was dynamite, dynamite, dynamite. Each evening the men played rougher and harder. Now it was camp policy that the only time that the Italians were permitted in the outhouse was during the day to clean up. But finally one night some of the guys took some Bery flare pistols out of the planes. Some joker fired a red one over the outhouse. Out came an Italian running and trying to hold onto his pants, which had dropped down to his ankles causing him to fall. He ran screaming, cursing, and praying all the while attempting to pull up his pants. No slapstick comedian could have put on a better show. He thought we were blowing up the outhouse with him in it. He ran down the road as the drunken guys kept shooting off their Bery pistols in his direction until he was out of sight. Evidently, he had thought that he could slip into the outhouse, use it, brag about his feat, and thus become a local legend. Well in reality, I guess he was some sort of a local legend.

My friend, Zal, who was with the ground troops in the first invasion of North Africa, Sicily, and did a "walk-through" of Italy and southern France told me this one. When his outfit established itself in southern Italy, they built a two-hole outhouse. Then they invited the mayor and the police chief of a nearby town to speak at the grand opening of the new facility. The townspeople also came along to join in the celebration. I had a picture of the mayor and the chief dressed in their uniforms. The mayor's outfit included his "Commodore Hornblower" hat and a sword at his side. Both men made their speeches, impressing the townspeople, and then cut the ribbon draped across the front of the structure. The men in the company, in the mean time, had drawn lots for the privilege of first use. At the appropriate time, two GIs dropped their pants and stepped into the outhouse. Their patsies, the two public officials, knew that they had been had and were highly insulted. On the other hand, when it all dawned on the townspeople as to what had happened, they went into uncontrollable laughter. It was probably the first laughter that they had had since Mussolini had taken them into the war. It all ended with the company CO apologizing to the town. Had this been done on a higher level, it could have created an international incident and the Italians my have changed sides again.

14

Heading for Home: June 1945

Cockpit of the B-24

By Emmett (Mac) MacKenzie

The Plane and Crew Assignment

In many ways, we were a lucky crew. We were replacement crew number 13. We also had a 13 in our crew number (313). So what is the significance of 13? In our day, it was supposed to be a very unlucky number. Roy recalls that when there a was a need, individual officers and enlisted men would elect to fly with us because they knew we were a lucky crew—lucky in that we had a well-trained crew and fortune smiled on us most favorably. Not only did we make it through our missions with just one injury but also we were fortunate enough to fly every place we went (except for short distances). This was our legacy as we prepared to depart Italy for home. Returning to Gioyia, our first touch down in Italy, we were debriefed before returning stateside. It was here that Jim remembers during his debriefing that he said he was from Missouri and at the same time General Johnson (Ploesti Air Raid participant) of the 15th Air Force passed by. On hearing that Jim was from his own home state, he called Jim over and began chatting away with him in an easy manner. After all, one had to recognize and speak to a fellow Missourian.

We were assigned to a B-24M in which to fly back to the U.S. It had undergone a careful inspection and repairs, and parts were replaced where necessary. When all was ready, the orders were cut and the crew that was assigned to it was comprised of Roy, Bill, Dave Feldman (our new navigator in the 461st), Paul, Jim, Lou, Byron, and me. In addition to us were two other flight officers. Finally, we were ready to depart Italy forever as a crew. We first made a test flight on June 3rd, taking two hours and forty-five minutes. On June 5th, we taxied on to the runway and took to the air towards Marrakech, Morocco.

Gioya, Italy to Marrakech, Africa

The first leg of our flight followed the northern tip of Africa flying over Sicily, Tunis, and Algeria landing in Marrakech, Africa, which was no more than 100 miles from the Atlantic Ocean. We covered this distance of approximately 1,600 miles in about 9 hours and 25 minutes if one calculates that our cruising speed of approximately 170 mph. It was a long day's flight and we were glad to get out of the plane and head for the showers, supper, and the sack. But for Paul and Jim, their day was not over. There were the usual post-light checks to make sure the mechanical, hydraulic, and electrical systems were functioning properly. Next was the task of refueling the plane, filling the "Main System," which was comprised of 12 cells and four systems holding a maximum of 2,343 U.S. gallons of 100 octane gasoline, depending on how much gasoline the four engines had consumed at cruising speed during the flight time, The Auxiliary Wing Tank System, comprising two systems, was topped off with 450 gallons. Hopefully, we would never have to depend on the auxiliary system to get us to our destination. Only after the refueling task was complete, did Paul and Jim clean up, eat, and relax.

Marrakech to Dakar, Senegal

The second leg was shorter covering a distance of 1,380 miles in approximately 8 hours and 10 minutes. I remember a ground person led us to our quarters. And as we carried our B-2 flight bags, I noticed the local workers passing by us. Most were of Arabic and African decent. One fellow in particular was a young man, slight of build, with the most piercing eyes I had every seen. He was the perfect stereotype of a person not to be trusted in or out of sight, I thought. Following mess, we were told there was going to be a prizefight that evening. It was June and the night was long in coming. Several of the crewmembers decided to go. It might be a lot of fun to watch. Seated near the ring, we saw two huge muscular black Senegalese men enter the ring. They were smiling down at the audience. No instructions of fair play were issued, just get in there and slug away. Finally the fight began. They waded into each other with one punishing blow followed by another. All the while, they seemed to be having the time of their lives. I don't remember who won the fight, but that was not the point. They and the audience were having a great time.

Trans-Atlantic Flight to Natal, Brazil

The next morning, we arose early had breakfast and headed for the flight line. Paul and Jim had already completed their preflight inspection, and we were ready to cross the Atlantic one more time. Our destination was Natal, Brazil, a distance of approximately 1,900 miles from

Dakar. It was going to be a long boring flight of about 11 hours. With all precautions taken for a safe flight, we taxied onto the runway and took off toward the southwest establishing a heading of 221 degrees. With luck we would land at Natal at approximately 5:30 P.M. having crossed one time zone and picking up an extra hour of daylight. For the most part the flight would be leisurely letting the autopilot do its thing. Roy and Bill took turns at the controls making sure that the engines were giving us the biggest bang for the buck. Dave kept track of our heading making sure we did not stray off course. And of course Lou had to spend time at the radio keeping in touch with both Dakar and Natal. Paul as usual had to make sure that the engines were operating efficiently, making sure fuel transfers were made when necessary and that the oil pressures were staying in the safe zone. The two returning officers spent most of their time in the waist with nothing to do. The waist of the plane then became the gathering place for conversation, card playing, and shooting the bull for those men taking breaks and the others with little or no responsibility on the return flight.

Only once did we have a problem. One of the engines quit on us. Radioing Dakar of our problem, we were asked if we wished to return. Roy's response was, "No thank you, we are going on. This crew has flown combat missions with just two engines and we are not about to turn around and come back." His response settled the discussion. Approaching Natal, the sky was overcast and it was raining but we landed without incident. I remember an Army truck came out to get us and some of our baggage. We were taken to the latest building concept to house transient returning airmen. The sleeping quarters were huts that stood at least 8 feet high feet off the ground resting on wooden posts driven into the ground. This whole base was primitive, located on the edge of a rain forest that was covered with dense vegetation. We stowed our gear, cleaned up, ate supper, and hit the sack. We were all tired after the long trip.

Belem, Brazil and the Shopping Spree

The next leg of our flight home from Natal to Belm was approximately 950 miles It was an uneventful flight flying over a mat of solid green until we reached the air base on the edge of the Araguaia river as it opened into the Atlantic Ocean, approximately 200 miles south of the mighty Amazon river. Once more we moved into a stilt city, and no wonder, considering the torrential rain. The weather was not good for flying the next morning so we laid over another day. Finally it stopped raining by early afternoon and we headed for town. As I remember, it was rather primitive. But primitive or not, commerce was thriving in Belem.

Since there were many crews returning to the states, there were dollars to be made off them en route home. There were numerous stores including specialty shops, leather goods, and arts and craft stores lining the muddy unpaved streets. Since we all had money to spend, we bought souvenirs to take home to our families. But one of the most intriguing stores was the shoe store. The prices were right—five bucks for a pair of boots 12 inches high. The boots looked and felt good when you put them on. Hardly a crewmember left without buying at least one pair. They were really great in dry weather. But after a few days subjected to damp or rainy weather, the soles deteriorated as if they were made of paper. The alternative was either having them resoled in the states or throwing them away. I elected to get mine resoled. I don't know what the other crewmembers did with theirs.

Puerto Rico—the Soft Life for Service Personnel

The-next-to-last leg of the flight ended at the Puerto Rico Naval Base. What a life for those stationed there and for returning aircrews—great tropical weather, blue skies, and much vegetation. The buildings were white stucco with red tile roofs. The dormitories were clean, spacious, airy and light. The cafeteria served great food. Outside the dormitory was a large swimming pool. And of course, officer and enlisted men's clubs were near by. To bad we only spent one night there.

The Final Touch Down—Macon, Georgia

Another 8 hours of flying time and 1,550 miles would mark the end of our journey. As we landed and headed to a parking area, I remember seeing many German prisoners-of-war wearing striped fatigues. It was a strange sight landing back in the US and seeing for the first time the men that had previously been the enemy. Having parked the plane, we all headed for a hanger where the enlisted men were relieved of all their wool dress greens, flight clothing, including Eisenhower and flight jackets, never to be seen again. In addition, we were relieved of our watches, binoculars, and 45s on threat of punishment if we tried to hide anything. Only the pilots, copilots, navigators, bombardiers, engineers, and radio operators were allowed to keep their watches. At the time, I didn't think it was fair at least not to be allowed to keep our watches.

Sioux Falls, South Dakota—Disbanding Crew No. 313

After having been briefed on the do's and don'ts, the enlisted men were issued new khaki uniforms and each man was given a month's furlough after which we were to report to the Sioux Falls Air Base. The original plan for our crew was to return from our furlough and begin training on B-29s and then to be shipped out to the Pacific Theatre of Operation. But August 8, 1945 was on us before we knew it, and Japan surrendered. Soon thereafter, individually we were assigned to other bases leading ultimately to discharge from the United States Army Air Corps. Only Roy, Bill, and I remained in the reserves for a period of time. However, the strangest thing about our crew's separation was that there was no attempt on anyone's part to get the crew together one last time for ol' time's sake. I guess we had just experienced too many events and had seen too much of each other every waking hour for a solid year. On a one-to-one basis, certain members of the crew did exchange addresses. Andy visited Jim in Columbia, Missouri on his way with his family to take a job in Texas. I saw Jim in 1950 as I was on my way to Selfridge Air Force Base in Michigan having been recalled to active duty for a year during the Korean War. Other than that, no member saw one another for 47 years until 1992. I was fortunate enough to have visited all the crewmembers at their homes or at the 376th annual Reunion, except for Guy.

Epilogue

If we could travel back in time for another crew portrait...

Tribute to "The Man"
By Emmett (Mac) MacKenzie

I would like to quote from the book, *The Soldier*, by Paul Perkins. The excerpt specifically refers to the pilot from the chapter entitled "The Air Crew:"

> The pilot was the airplane commander; the B-24 and crew were his charges. He was responsible for the safety and efficiency of the crew at all times—not just when flying and fighting, but for the full twenty-

four hours of every day he was in command. How well each crew-member contributed as a member of the combat team greatly depended on the command skill of the pilot. The pilot needed to know each member of the crew as an individual and take a personal interest in him. Like the commander of any force, large or small, he set the tone for morale. Success as airplane commander was grounded in the respect, confidence, and trust the crew had for him. The respect needed to be for him as an individual—not the position he held. He needed to understand his job and duty—and to convince the crew that he knows his stuff. The pilot needed to be friendly, and understanding, but firm. He had to be fair and impartial in his decisions. The decision—once made—had to be final. Crew discipline bred comradeship and high morale as a natural by-product. The airplane commander was coach in a sport with mortal stakes.

While the above depiction of a command pilot is the ideal, Roy A. Hatem, our pilot, most closely fit the description of the true command pilot. Not only was he one of the best pilots in the 514th, the crew trusted him with their lives. He paired off and cross-trained crew members so that each pair could perform one another's job. He had the will and determination to fly his missions and to return home safely. Without this single-minded purposefulness, our crew might never have made it back and lived to talk about their adventures 47 years later. As Paul O'Steen once said after being interviewed for the job of Flight Engineer (Charleston Air Base, July, 1944) "Hey, this guy is coming back, so I'm flying with him."

Memories and Nostalgia: A Tribute to Our Crew
By Michael Oczkus

We as a crew survived because that one fatal gun wasn't there. However, the crew had a great deal to do with our survival. Barring none, we had the best crew going where each did his work regardless of the danger involved. We could count on each other and we all came through. There is lot more but I'll leave it to others to tell. All that I have written is as I have remembered it. There were many in-flight events that went on in the waist that those of us in the nose weren't aware that happened and vice versa. One time in the nose I passed out four times from lack of oxygen. I kept pulling my oxygen mask hose out of the oxygen supply line. When I failed to respond to the Roy on a request, he asked Mac to get out of the nose turret and find out what was wrong. He left the nose turret four times to re-hook me up with oxygen, in fact saving my life. Probably nobody in the waist was aware of this.

In conclusion, Charles Dickens can best sum up my personal feelings about the war in his English classic story of *A Tale of Two Cities*. "It was the best of times and it was the worst of times." And that's the way it was for me. It was the best of times and it was the worst of times.

THE END

Definitions

Air speed: The speed of the plane relative to the speed of the air. Critical factors included flight altitudes, the variable and directional winds, and the weather conditions over the Italian, Austrian, and Yugoslavian Alps.

Box formation: A flight formation that a squadron flies. A is the lead drop-bombing plane. Planes B & C fly the same altitude as A and on each side of A. Plane D flies below and at a safe distance from the other planes to avoid their prop wash. This pattern is duplicated for additional squadrons.

```
                A
        B               C
                D
        E               F       (as needed)
```

Ground speed: The distance covered with respect to the ground. This was not used as a measure of the distance to the target on the ground.

Flight time: The time the plane was in the air. The calculation included such factors as the time consumed for each plane to rendezvous with the other planes of the squadron, group, or wing of the flight organization. The recording of flight time began when the wheels were in stored position within the plane's wings at takeoff and ended when the wheels were extended and locked on touching the ground on landing.

Initial (heading) point (IP): The location where a flight of planes rendezvoused and then flew directly to the target.

Mission: A special assignment given to a military group.

Mission credit: Each crewmember was awarded one point for each target (or alternate target) successfully bombed. Fifty points were needed to fulfill the requirements set by the 15th Army Air Force for homebound rotation.

PFF: Path Finder Fix radar. The radar could see through clouds and under-cast. It was located in what was formerly the location of the Sperry Ball Turret. A trained Radar Navigational Operator dropped bombs from the lead ship of the flight and the other planes in the box would follow suit.

Sortie: A flight of combat aircraft on a mission.

Sortie credit: One point was awarded each man toward fulfilling the requirements of the mission depending on variables involved such as distance and time. The flight was considered to be one or two sorties. The criteria used to establish the number of sorties depended on the mission, but they were not always apparent to the crew, at least not to the enlisted men.

Bibliography

"Christmas" by Joe Aberwald, *Stars and Stripes*, January 1945.

"Flight Dairy," by Paul O'Steen, November 1944 thru April, 1945—Paul O'Steen

"Stories" by Bill Roberts, *Orlando Press*, 1963

Flight Manual B-24D Airplane, September 15, 1942, Aviation Publications, 217 E. Washington St., P.O. Box 357, Appleton, WI, 54912-0357.

Form 5 Flight Records (recollections and personal records of crewmembers)

Founding Units, by James W. Walker, published by the 376th Heavy Bombardment Group

Capri, Interdipress S.N.C. Napoli, Edito e stampato dalla, Villa, Plurigraf, Narni–Terni 1983

Liberator, Consolidated Vultee, General Dynamics in Celebration of the 50th Anniversary of the B-24 General Dynamics, Convair Division Liberator, San Diego, CA, December 29, 1989.

National Geographic, Vol. 165. No. 5, May 1984.

The Liberandos: A World War II History of the 376th Bomb Group H and its Founding Units, James W. Walker, 376th Heavy Bombardment Group, Veterans Association, Inc., 1994.

The Log of the Liberator, by Steve Birdsall, John Preston, illustrator. Doubleday & Co, 1973.

Crew Biographies
By Emmett (Mac) MacKenzie

Bill Anclam, Copilot
1921–

Bill grew up in Janesville, Wisconsin, played high school football and after graduating from high school, was eventually employed by the Parker Pen Company in Janesville. He married June, his high school sweet heart and friend. But as war went on and posters could be found everywhere advertising "Uncle Sam Wants You!" Bill read the Army Air Corps ads and radio propaganda proclaiming the advantages of joining up. He was bitten by the bug. Even though he was married man, he wanted to become a fighter pilot for the thrill of it—besides the desire to serve his country. June consented. He met all the requirements for Officers Candidate School (OCS) and, after finishing basic training, he was sent to the Army Air Corps ground school and basic flight training school. When he finished that and intermediate flight training, he was eager and ready to complete advanced fighter pilot school. He knew that he had found his niche in the Air Corps. But as fate would have it, Bill was destined to pursue another path.

The volume of B-24s being produced put pressure on the Air Corps to push the B-24 pilot training program to produce pilots to man the planes, and now there was a shortage of co-pilots. Therefore, the Air Corps restricted the training of fighter pilots and sent these trainees through a crash course for B-24 copilots. Unfortunately, Bill was one of the men. He was not happy warrior but took what fate had handed him and became a reluctant but a good copilot at the age of 24.

Bill was also a strong and ruggedly built blond-haired man, just the type needed to help fly a B-24. If something were to happen to Roy, the crew knew that Bill could get us back to base if the plane was flyable. In general, he was a happy-go-lucky guy; always ready for a good prank to play when the opportunity presented itself. He was well-liked by the other officers as well as the enlisted men. During the crew's time together, he and Paul developed a special bond of friendship.

At war's end, Bill had been promoted to a First Lieutenant, and on separation from the Air Force, he returned home to June and the job he had at the Parker Pen Co. Then he and June started their family with two girls. But he still wanted to fly, so he joined the Air Force Reserve unit, which was close Janesville. This unit had no planes to fly so after several months, Bill dropped out. The only other air reserve unit was a great distance from Janesville, so Bill gave up and returned to his favorite sports of fishing and hunting which he pursued for many years with his black Labrador dog. But the days of fishing and hunting now are over and Bill has found that the local pool hall is a sufficient challenge for his talents. Bill is now content to live the quiet life with June and share their lives with their daughters and grand children. And of course, there is his faithful black Labrador hunting dog.

Guy Bretilotte, Warrant Officer
1922–March 1997

Guy was somewhat of a laid-back sort of a guy. However, he took his work seriously, studying maps and charts in preparation for each mission. He also knew well the job requirements of an ordinance and armament specialist. As the crew's bombardier, he knew that he probably would be responsible for the accidental death of some civilians. The thought of this probability was always with him.

Guy grew up in a small Iowa town. He had graduated from college and was about to enter a career in business when he decided to volunteer for the Army Air Force. He would like to have become a pilot. But for some reason or other, he did not qualify. But he did qualify to become a bombardier, which, as it turned out, fitted his talents most closely. Guy was promoted to a 2nd Lt. by the end of the war

Guy was no eager beaver as were Roy and Mike. He preferred to take it easy. Many were the times when he would lounge in the waist or in the nose area of the plane appearing to be sleeping. But he was probably going over the upcoming mission in his mind and considering the bomb run. He also had to consider the lack of lateral maneuverability while making the bomb run if he were bombing a marshalling yard located in narrow valley such as Innsbruck, Austria, The minute but critical adjustments to the Sperry Bomb sight was required of him before releasing his bombs, especially if he was the lead bombardier for the Squadron that day. After the war, he entered the business world and became a Commodities International Broker until his death in March 1997.

Lou Birnbaum, Radio Operator
March 31, 1925–

In 1941, Lou attended school in Philadelphia, PA. He was not overly interested in school and certainly not in college. At the time, it was just too much of an economic and social reach for him. But for some reason or other, he was interested in observing the words and actions of his parents and much older siblings. He was the eleventh and last child to be born to Herman and Fannie Birnbaum. His parents had come to the US in 1920 searching for a better life. Because of the difference in his age compared to that of his brothers and sisters, he did not feel the closeness that otherwise he might have felt for them. The opportunity did not exist for sharing common experiences. Times being what they were and the need to make a living, Lou quit high school and studied upholstering. It was during this time that he really became aware of the value system that was beginning to take shape in his life. One of these values was the importance of physical fitness to a person's well-being. Lou joined Inky's Gym with some of his buddies and continued to pump iron after they were no longer interested and had stopped. At the age of 57, he got serious about exercising again and joined a spa. He goes to the spa three times a week in the firm belief that one can still build muscle even when one is over 60.

Living in North Philadelphia, Lou and his buddies would go somewhere else for their entertainment. That somewhere was South Philadelphia. The entertainment was the synagogue dances. It was here, in 1938, that Lou met Anne. Lou was 13 and Anne was 11 years old. They both liked to dance, and that's how their relationship began—on the dance floor. In addition to dancing, they both liked to swim. For five years thereafter, they continued to date going to parties and dances until Lou was inducted into the service. Thereafter, they continued to correspond every week until he returned home after the war.

Lou was 18 when he was drafted into the service and had the distinction of being the youngest person to be drafted from his neighborhood. During one of the military job placement interviews, he was asked if he would like to fly. He thought the offer over and decided that it would beat being a foot soldier so he accepted the offer. After basic training, he attended radio operators' school at Sioux Falls, South Dakota and gunnery school at Yuma, Arizona. After graduating from these schools, he was sent to Westover Air Base where our crew would be formed in July 1944. Returning to the US at the close of the European theater operation on June 18, 1945, he was sent to Sioux Falls Air Base for reassignment. After receiving a month's furlough, however, on August 14, 1945, the Japanese surrendered and the war was over. Then Lou was sent to Amarillo, Texas and was discharged in October of 1945 having served 26 months in the Army Air Corps.

Picking up where he left off before the war, Lou returned to his chosen trade and finished his apprenticeship in the field of interior decorating making draperies and slip covers. He married Anne in 1946 and in 1947 completed his high school credits and received his diploma. But Lou remained uncertain about his career and decided to try the insurance business in 1948. He entered the training program for the position of an insurance agent with Metropolitan Life. At that time,

Lou thought the best thing to do was to give answers to test questions that would satisfy the company but not those that he really believed. He thought this was what one had to do to make it in the business world. But this response was destined early on to come in conflict with his true beliefs. On the social level, he felt uncomfortable being an insurance agent especially when he was with his friends. They thought that all he wanted to do was to sell them an insurance policy. This disturbed him. Secondly, having spent much time and effort going over an insurance program with a prospective customer, the answer he received at closure time was all too often, "No!" Not being able to take this response time after time, he left the job of salesman to those with thicker skins and perhaps a less discriminating conscience.

In 1949 Lou joined an older brother in opening a decorating business that lasted into 1954. Meanwhile, Lou and Anne's first child, Dona, was born in 1951. He took a job as foreman for a boat seat manufacturing company and worked there through 1955. It was during 1952 that Lou began to wonder and become curious about college life—what was it all about, was he missing something, and what was there to learn? To answer these questions, he enrolled at Temple University and took various courses. He came to realize that college was just part of life's experiences and not to be held in awe. Enlightened with this knowledge, he left college never to return. It wasn't until 1956 that Lou established himself as the founder and owner of his own interior decorating company. His son, Eric, was born in 1957 and is now a practicing lawyer in Philadelphia. Several years after founding his business, Lou joined his nephew as a partner. The partnership lasted until 1987. He retired in 1989 and moved to Lake Worth, Florida. Another tenant of Lou's value system beliefs as a tradesman was: Do it right to the best of your ability so that you won't embarrass yourself or be criticized for lack of professional ability. It's a matter of personal integrity and honor that is at stake. He learned this from his father and has always been tough on himself. He also instilled these beliefs in his children. This same philosophy was extended to his employees who he encouraged to put forth their best effort to do a good job so that they would be a credit to themselves as well as being a valued employee.

Lou has set out two goals that he hopes to achieve in the remainder of his life: "First, I want to be a good bridge player, and second, I want to be a good golfer." Lou's character and strong beliefs are a part of the 10 reasons that Crew 313 was the best there was.

Andre Duval, Belly Gunner
September 14, 1925–

> *Author's Note: Andy submitted this autobiography.*

For my first 18 years, I lived in South Hadley, Massachusetts; one of three children—a sister who died in 1984 and a brother who is now a retired dentist. We as a family were financially poor but rich with love and care. I attended local schools and after the first year of high school, I entered and completed a 3-year trade school majoring in the electrical trade.

President Truman summoned me to join the Army Air Corps so I reported to Ft. Devens on February 14, 1944. From there I was sent to Greensboro, North Carolina for basic training and for psycho-motive tests as I requested pilot training. As it turned out, my score was below those who went on to pilot training, thus, I was sent to Harlingen, Texas to gunnery school. Gunnery training was enjoyable and I excelled.

Immediately following gunnery school, I arrived at Westover Field and was assigned to Heavy Bomber Group and Crew No. 313 with Lt. Hatem as pilot. Not knowing it at the time, this turned out to be a perfect assignment with the best possible crew. As a crew (with a feeling of togetherness), we trained in Charleston, South Carolina, then went on to San Pangrazio, Italy by way of Mitchell Fields, New York; Bangor, Maine; Gander Air Base, Newfoundland; Azores; Marrakech, French Morocco; Tunisia; Garcia, Italy; and then to San Pangrazio, Italy—the location of the 514th Squadron and the 376th Heavy Bomb Group. There we continued in togetherness as a crew. Ten fine men.

Now, for the rest of the story as a civilian. For the first year after returning states-side, I worked at repairing clocks. Then I entered Wilbraham Academy in Wilbraham, Massachusetts as a boarding student and completed high school. Jeannette and I were married on August 16, 1947. I entered the freshman class at Clarkson University in Potsdam, New York in September 1947. Jeannette was an RN and worked part time in Potsdam. During the four years at Clarkson University, we had our first two children. In June of 1951, I received a Bachelor of Science Degree in Electrical Engineering. Jeannette, the two girls, and I moved to Texas and we purchased a home in Arlington. I was employed as an engineer at Chance Vought Aircraft. My work involved analysis, design, and the testing of guidance and controls for Navy missiles, the Regulus I and Supersonic Regulus II auto-pilot. We grew to like Texas very much. While in Arlington, I became active in the Junior Chamber of Commerce and attained a title of Vice President. In June, 1957, we moved to Orlando, Florida where I became employed by Martin Marietta Corp. Again, my work involved analysis, design tests, and flight tests of missiles such as the Lacrosse, Sprint, SAM-D/Patriot, and the Pershing. In later years I was made Systems Engineering Department Manager. Following this, I became the Systems Engineering Manager for the LANTERN program. During the early years in Orlando, we had our last two children for a total of four—three girls and one boy—Andrea, Lynn, Dean, and David. They are also grandparents to Allen Adams, Nicole, Michael, Kelly, and Tracy Dunham.

I chose to retire in May 1988. My career was enviable and enjoyable. I can look back at having had a dream come true in 1972 when we purchased an ocean-front condominium at New Smyrna Beach, Florida and we continue to use it as a get-away from Orlando. On January 5, 1994, I started an IRS-sponsored tax preparation course in order to become an AARP volunteer for Senior Citizens.

Jeannette and I very much enjoyed meeting and sharing the fellowship that ensued with Roy and Marilyn, Emmett and Pauline, Lou and Anne, and Jim at the 376th Heavy Bomb Group convention. Jeannette is already looking for western-wear for the trip to Austin, TX next September 1997.

Roy Hatem, Pilot
August 30, 1918–January 24, 2002

Roy's home was New York City. He was a gong-ho young man in his early years, a stocky and strong, which was to serve him well in the future. He joined the Army National Guard and gave his age as 18. He was assigned to the 69th Regiment. He joined the New York Police Force in 1940 and remained with the organization until being unable to withstand the urge to serve his country, he join the Army Air Force and was sent to Officers Candidate School. Although a married man, he directed all his energy to becoming the best B-24 pilot in his class. He completed ground and flight training courses, and graduated from advanced B-24 pilot school. He received his 'wings' and was commissioned a 1st Lt. 1943.

His strong will and determination to return to his wife, Dorothy, and his yet-unborn son was a built-in insurance policy that the crewmembers would return home intact. He was 26 when the crew was formed. He was relentless in his pursuit to master all the technical details required to be a B-24 pilot. In short, he was a perfectionist. He demanded much of himself and of those who served under him. Roy had all the physical qualities that would serve him well when piloting the not-so-easy-to-fly B-24. No doubt about it, Roy was a self-made man, always striving to be the best regardless of the job he had undertaken, and he expected the people with whom he worked to be just as dedicated as he was.

A lighter side of Roy was his love for singing over the intercom with Lou, the radio operator, after having successfully made it through another mission. Some of their favorites were "Lilly Marlene," "I'm a Yankee Doodle Dandy" and "I Want a Paper Doll that I can Call My Own."

When Roy was assigned a crew, he worked with the new flight engineer trying to help him to get up to speed and learn his job, which he should have already known but apparently didn't. The flight engineer's job was crucial for the welfare of the crew. So after working with the guy a week, Roy determined that this man was not going to work out. Roy needed someone that knew the job and on whom he could depend. Then along came Paul who was waiting for a crew assignment as a flight engineer. After Paul and Roy talked about the job, Roy could tell that Paul had the job skills. Both men knew their job assignment and when Roy told Paul he was coming back to his wife and child, Paul said, "I'm with you!" That clinched the deal. Paul was made the crew-chief for Crew No. 313.

As for Roy's family life, he and Dorothy, his first wife, started their family before the crew flew overseas. Their first son, Roy Junior, was born while Roy was stationed in Italy. It wasn't until 1947 that John George was born, followed by Dorothy Ann the next year.

Mean while, Roy had returned to his job as a lieutenant with the New York Police Department and became the Assistant Chief of Police before retiring in 1965. But in 1963, Dorothy died and he was lonely. Roy was fortunate enough to have met Marilyn, herself a widow, who had three children also—Marilyn, Patrick, and Theresa. Marilyn became the love of Roy's life. She was gracious, sharp, witty, and a delightful person to be around. Roy and Marilyn were wed in 1966 and the two families became one with 8 members.

The same year that Roy retired from the NYPD, he contacted his sources in the State Department and got a job with the Public Safety Division. He went on to become an advisor to police departments in Vietnam, Korea, and Zaire. This activity was followed by an assignment to Washington DC. He wrote a procedure to be followed by law enforcement authorities in case of terrorist attach. The plan was approved and implemented.

Ever restless to find something in a related field of activity, Roy again became a public safety consultant to foreign countries and to the Department of Interior and Indian tribes for the next three years. Finally, to use Roy's own words, "I got fed up with police work."

But this was not the end of Roy's work life. He became a real estate broker and salesman in Florida from 1979 through 1986 when he retired and started playing golf on the course just beyond his backyard in Sun City, Florida.

Roy was always at his best when he could take on the role of the devils advocate. He loved to argue politics or any other subject that presented a challenge to his way of thinking. All a person had to do was to realize that this was entertainment in Roy's way of thinking and play the game with him inserting apposing ideas. If he was involved in a contentious situation and he thought there was an injustice about to be committed, he wasn't about to let the injustice go unchallenged. I remember one such time when five members of the crew were gathered at a reunion luncheon for the 376th in September 1992. Jim Snell, our top turret gunner, had a problem with diverticulitis and of necessity was a vegetarian. The waiter for our table said he didn't have anything that Jim could eat. That sent up the red flag for Roy. "What do you mean there's no food for this man to eat? If you can't find a salad or something similar, I'll go back to the kitchen myself and get in the face of the manager and get what he can eat." With that pronouncement, it wasn't more than five minutes until Jim was handed the food that he needed and wanted.

It was probably March or April, 1992 after all members of our crew were accounted for and talking on the phone to each other after 47 years of silence that Roy wrote me a note which I will always prize as true Roy-ism:

> Mac, maybe if and when we all get together, my memory will be refreshed, as it was during that long phone call of ours. I was luckier than most of you when we had our adventures. You poor guys had to sweat it out in your various stations while I was up to my ears trying to get us home and too damned busy to think of anything else. I don't know how I would reacted to just being unable to do anything but hope to God that the ass flying the plane knew what they were doing or at least guessed at what to do right. It took guts to sit there and take it. I think that I'd have gone nuts having to rely on someone else, especially someone like me who was half nuts. Thank God that He was around when we needed Him. But it was a great experience.

Byron Hunsicker Jr., Tail Gunner
April 29, 1924–April 29, 1993

Byron A. Hunsicker Jr. Was born in Willoughby, Ohio. His wife, Delores; two children, Byron A. Hunsicker III and Christine Beck; two grandchildren, Terra Hunsicker and Marcia Hunsicker; and a brother survive him. (Byron was not the Byron "II" because this title is always reserved for the son of the brother if the brother has a son. Therefore Byron Jr.'s (Our Byron's) son is Byron Hunsicker III. Delores, Byron's wife, made sure that I knew the difference between the IIs and the IIIs.)

Jim and I (Mac) had planed to go to the US Air Force Museum in Dayton, Ohio. We knew that Byron didn't have much longer to live so we made a special effort to see his and his wife in Mentor Ohio. It was a good thing we did because he died three days after we visited him in the hospital. It was the first time and the last time that all three men had seen each together since 1945. I had just finished making a plastic model of a B-24J, which Jim and I gave to Byron. As soon as Byron saw it, he asked the nurse to hang it up where he could see it. Surprisingly, he seemed to enjoy our visit with him. This helped him to make his day a little better.

Not much is known by our crew members regarding Byron's early days as a teenager accept that he was an outstanding basketball player in high school. In one game when Byron's team, the Rangers, was playing the Ashtabula Panthers, it was a fast and furious game. The *Willoughby Gazette* ran an article on it titled "Double Trouble:"

> As an illustration of how fast the game was being played, Byron Hunsicker was the high score man until he made the error of trying to shoot a basket for Ashtabula. As he got set for the shot his teammates shouted to him but the ball left his hands and sailed for the bucket. It was the only time during the evening that the fans hoped that "Honey" Byron Jr. wouldn't make a basket. Fortunately for Willoughby, he missed.

Byron was a self-confident, unassuming, with a pleasant disposition, and a quiet guy with a mind of his own. He will always be remembered as the handsome, dark-haired guy who literally protected our tails when flying sorties and missions over Italy, Yugoslavia, Germany, and Austria. He was always a vigilant protector of his crew's safety. One time he spotted a German ME-109 fighter plane and served notice with his 50 caliber machine guns that it should not come within the range of our plane. The fighter left the scene. On another occasion, he spotted a German-captured B-24 following our formation, reported its presence to Roy, and kept a wary eye on its activities until it disappeared. (At that time, the Germans were merely tracking our target heading.) Byron flew 26 missions with our crew.

While on R & R on the island of Capri, there was a contingent of young Women Air Corps women whom Byron and Paul encountered. That made for an enjoyable time. So you see the island had other attractions other than mountains and Roman ruins.

On returning to the states and prior to Byron's discharge from the Army Air Corps in 1945, he was promoted to the rank of a Tech Sergeant specializing in armament. However, he had failed to communicate with Delores during this time. Then out of the blue, he received the following tersely stated message, "Are YOU dead or just plain disinterested?" It was as if a bomb had exploded in his head. He had just assumed that all was well. But now he knew that it wasn't. In a flash, Byron took decisive action. He put on his best dress uniform with his chest decorated with service ribbons, including those received from the Italian campaign, marched into the CO's office, and told him that he needed to go home and get married. The CO gave Byron the furlough to go home and get married, feeling empathy for an Army Air Corps veteran. Delores and Byron were married on October 11th, 1945. Both returned to Randolph Air Base, Virginia. But Byron was not discharged as soon as he would have liked. Because he could read and write, he was given the job of processing and discharging fellow airmen until October 29th at which time he was discharged and allowed to return home. In the mean time, Delores had returned home.

Byron followed shortly thereafter having received an honorable discharge. He was the only enlisted man, outside of Paul O'Steen, and Lou Birnbaum to have achieved military rank of Tech Sergeant among the enlisted men.

Because Byron had elected to stay on reserve status, he was called back to active duty in 1950 for seven days at the end of which time the US Air Force let him return home without a discharge certificate. No one seemed to know the logic of his recall orders. However, in the mix-up, Byron never did receive a discharge for that short period of active duty in 1950, so it may be rightfully assumed that he is still on active duty in the Air Force.

Byron enrolled at Case Institute of Technology, Western Reserve University between 1947 and 1949. Delores helped to keep food on the table by getting a city job of maintaining cemetery records. She felt that Byron was sometimes too preoccupied with shooting pool at his frat house to help out with the finances, so Delores got him a real down-to-earth job digging grave sites to help out with the expenses. By 1949, Byron III was on the way and without sufficient funds to support the new family members, Byron quit school and went to work for the Hamonn Construction Co. Delores and Byron's daughter was born in 1951 and his family was complete. He stayed with the construction company 15 years and was well liked by Mr. Hamonn, the company owner. He advanced in his chosen trade and supervised the building of many structures. At the end of this period of his life, Byron went out and started a construction company of his own for several years. However, the economy turned sour and he was forced to liquidate his business. Thereafter, he worked again for Hamonn and other construction companies over a period of many years. It was said that he was the best project cost estimator in the business supervising the erecting of many buildings in the Midwest, eastern, and southern parts of the country.

For the family, one of Byron's most lasting imprints on the local landscape is a middle school that he built. His son presently teaches there and his grandchildren are or will be attending school in the building that their grandfather built.

Probably the personal quality that most typified Byron's life was the special attention that he gave to the details of his work. Once when attending a concert with Delores, she found him pondering over the fresco designs on the walls rather than being enchanted by the music. On another occasion, he happened to be in a church and he commented to Delores, "You know, that cross on the wall isn't straight, it's tilted." In retrospect, maybe it was tilted, tilted toward Byron.

Emmett (Mac) MacKenzie, Nose Gunner
May 23, 1923–

I was born May 23, 1923 in Denver, Colorado. My birth record gives my name as Emmett Edward Graham Jr. My mother died when I was five months old. The court system took me and my twin sisters away from my father because he had tuberculosis and could not support the family. My sisters and I were placed in different institutions for homeless children, my sisters being placed in the same place. I was adopted at age 4-1/2 years by my foster family that had cared for me since I was 18 months old.

I had many good childhood experiences while growing up. My adopted mother and father both worked. The Great Depression years were very hard on the family. My Dad only earned $100 a month and my Mom $23 a month. I actually was raised by my grandmother who lived our home.

I graduated from high school in 1941 and worked a year to earn money to attend college at the University of Colorado in August 1942. I joined the Air Force Reserve program in the fall of the same year and was called to active duty in April 1943. The group of men that I was with was supposed to get basic training for 8 weeks at Seymore Johnson Air Base in North Carolina. The training was extended to 12 weeks and finally to 16 weeks. It was one of those Air Corp glitches: "What shall we do with these soldiers?" Seymore was the same base that Paul was training to be an aircraft mechanic.

I attended Aircraft Mechanics School at the same base for six weeks before taking the Officers Candidate School test. I passed both the written and physical tests. From there I was sent to Maxwell Air Base for further screening. During the interview, I asked the officer for navigation training. But the school was closed. I told the interviewer that I was not interested in anything else so that was the end of OCS for me. After that let down, I was assigned to be trained in Aircraft Armament.

On the way to Armament School located at Buckley Air Base in Denver, Colorado, I met a fellow who would become my best friend in the service, Charlie Thacker. Following graduation, we were both sent to Gunnery School at Tyndall Air Base in Florida. Charlie was washed out because he was color blind. Ironically, in civilian life, he became a much sought after color photographer specializing in weddings.

On completion of gunnery school, I was sent to Westover Air Base in Hadley Falls, Massachusetts for assignment to an aircrew. After only becoming acquainted with my new air crew for a few hours, I was given a two-week leave. On returning home to Denver, I went to the local airport, Stapleton Field, and took flying lessons. Before returning to Westover, I had learned to fly and had soloed in a Piper Cub. Having time to reflect on the qualities of the new crew, I had a funny feeling about the members. They seemed to lack vitality, energy, and a will to survive. The day that I was to ship out with this crew, I didn't feel well and stopped by the infirmary and asked for a couple of aspirin. The medic took my temperature. It was 106 degrees. I was promptly hauled off to the hospital where I was confined to bed and was fed intravenously for three days of my seven-day stay. It was a welcomed relief to be there. I had come down with food poisoning. After my release from the hospital, I was assigned to Roy's crew. It was the best think that ever happened to me. My vibes told me this was going to be a good crew.

Following the war, I returned to Denver, remained in the Air Force Reserve, and got back in time to enroll in the fall quarter of 1945 at Colorado University. I graduated in 1949 with a BA in education and taught in the little mountain town of Yampa, Colorado near Steamboat Springs. I was involved in everything from teaching mathematics to elementary school gym classes, high school band, and assistant basketball coach.

One day I witnessed the best knock-down, drag-out, free-for-all, nose-bleeding, fist fight I have every seen in my life. It was between the Oak Creek miners and the Yampa farmers. The fight was over a bottle of whiskey that the miners accused the farmers of breaking. The fight had a fitting location, the school gymnasium, of course. Just like in the movies!

In the summer of 1950, I enrolled at Greeley State Teachers College to begin work on a master's degree in education. I had gotten a contract to teach that fall in a public school in Littleton, a suburb of Denver, when the fickle finger of fate once again touched me. "You are hereby ordered to report for duty to Cheyenne Air Force Base, Wyoming, for a period of one year as of October 10th 1950." Once there, I was given the opportunity of joining a B-29 crew as the Fire Control non-commissioned officer and fly missions over Korea. Having considered the idea for a couple of seconds, I thought better of the opportunity and turned it down.

Ultimately, I was assigned duty with Air Sea Rescue Service at Selfridge Air Force Base in Mount Clements, Michigan, a suburb of Detroit. It was a good year having become a friend of a local airman, George Johnson, and spent many weekends with George's family.

I had a non-com status of a Staff Sergeant, which entitled me to a private room in an enlisted men's barracks. One day during off duty hours, I bought a 1950 black Mercury coupe for transportation for a mere $1,750. Detroit was having a recession making the car quite cheap. Occasionally, I went with some other airmen, drinking only gin and 7Up at local a bar in Mt. Clements.

Before being discharged in 1951, I had sent an application to the Denver Public Schools. When I got back home, I went to the teacher's employment office. The guy that was doing the interviewing for a math teacher had had my application with three others on top of his desk attempting to decide on a last minute replacement starting the next day. He said he also had just been released from Selfridge Air Force base a month prior to this time. The next day, September 7, I began teaching at North High School in Denver.

I taught every math course from Basic Math through Calculus during the years 1951 to 1982. The math club that I sponsored received a National Science Foundation Science Fair recognition for building the first Analogue Computer in the school system and the city in 1957. A large part of the credit went to an undiscovered genius, Lester Belamey. I found him enrolled in General Mathematics instead of Advanced Algebra. Along with the other revved-up kids, we worked many mornings before school to get the project done in time for the November fair. Lester went on to become a Nuclear Physicist.

I married Pauline Johansen on June 11, 1955. She was an English teacher at North High. As the years passed, we had three girls: Ruth, born 1957; Robin, born 1960; and Rebecca, born 1964.

In the summer of 1960 I received an offer to work summers as a programmer for the National Bureau of Standards in Boulder, Colorado. I received my Master of Basic Science degree (Mathematics) in 1961. I owe much to Pauline for her unending support and encouragement. This employment lasted from 1961 to 1966 at which time president Lyndon B Johnson cut summer employment federal pay rolls.

In the fall of 1966, I accepted another offer to teach a 5-hour, Friday-night class to the brightest kids in the Denver Public Schools. They were some of the most brilliant people I have ever known and had the opportunity to work with. Their IQs ranged from 125 to 175. The program lasted 10 years and was a real challenge. Basic, Fortran, and Pascal computer languages with mathematical applications were the standard menu languages offered in all the six high schools. I also moonlighted at a local community college teaching Introduction to Data Processing for four years, 1976–1980. After 1966, I spent summers working odd jobs. The best was when I worked for a good friend, Don Ellery. He was a project superintendent for Stearns Rogers Mechanical Contracting Company. The large mining construction projects were located in Colorado and Arizona. Finally I decided to retire from teaching in 1962. Thirty two years was enough!

The John F. Kennedy High School math department honored me with a going away party and gifts. But the best tribute came from the student teacher from one of my early years, Jerry Hulstrom, who said he had always tried to emulate the teaching practices of his mentor.

For the next year and half, I went back to college for fun taking several courses in designing Passive Solar homes. Another enjoyable course was water colors.

In 1978 my daughters started to migrate to the Twin Cities, Minnesota. First Ruth who is now a professional singer; then Robin, who has become a banker; and finally Rebecca, who found employment at Sun Country Air Lines based in Minneapolis.

Once again the opportunity was presented to me to have another career. With some connections at Sperry Univac Computer Corporation, I was offered a job to write software computer manuals for the Stealth Bomber project on which the company was bidding. The company moved my family to Eagan, Minnesota, home of the company's headquarters. After 3 months on the job, Sperry lost the contract. After that I taught software computer modules to Air Traffic Control personnel located in Hawaii, Anchorage, and Atlantic City. From 1986 to 1989, I worked as a computer security specialist, overseeing the security of classified computers—hush, hush, and all that sort of stuff.

Unisys, formerly Sperry Univac, offered its employees a buy-out plan. I decided to take advantage of the program and was ready to retire for good on December 1, 1989. For the first three years after retiring, I served on the Mall of America Religious Council, The Eastern Lutheran Church Council and for nine years on the Board of Directors of the

Eagan Scholarship Foundation, Inc., a nonprofit organization charged with providing scholarships to graduating Eagan High School students as well as for three other high schools. It was hard work but was worth every minute of it.

As probably was true for all of us crew members, life was not always easy, but life has been rewarding for me.

Paul O'Steen, Flight Engineer
January 24, 1922–November 7, 1993

It cannot be said that Paul let grass grow under his feet. After having been discharged from the Air Force on Oct 1, 1945, he tried several jobs before he hit on one that he thought was right for him. First Paul tried working as a lumberjack in 1945. The job didn't last long. As he said, "I got out of that job to stay alive. It was a quick way to get killed." In 1946, he tried his hand at becoming a construction electrician, but after three years, he got board with the job. "Nothing exciting about that, just a lot of hard work."

Then in May 1949, Paul decided to go to work for the Los Angeles Police Department, mostly for job security, a pension, vacations, and health insurance. He spent 15 years on the job before the police department promoted him to detective. By 1978, he had become a supervisor of detectives for the homicide detail at the Hollywood Division.

In the mean time, Paul had married and became the father of Paul E. O'Steen Jr. in 1962. But as year passed by, the demands of police work took its toll on his marriage.

One day in 1978, Paul found himself in the restaurant across the street from division headquarters. While sitting in a booth, he and a fellow officer talked about the future. Paul had put in 29 years with the department and had had it with the police force. His friend had the same thoughts. It only took them the time to cross the street to headquarters, turn in their badges and guns, and to resign from the force making both free men

First he moved out of Los Angeles and went to South Lake Tahoe, California. Shortly thereafter, he met Shirlene, married her, and bought a house in Coarsegold, California, and lived there happily until his death in 1993.

The following is pure fantasy but it can serve to typify Paul's philosophy toward life and death:

> In the early morning hours of November 7, Ol' Boomerang quietly appeared over the horizon. Paul looked up and saw her circling overhead. Byron was waving out the waist window, beckoning Paul to join him. With that, Ol' Boomerang swooped down and landed near him. Paul thought to himself, "Oh, what the heck, I have seen everything and accomplished most everything that I wanted to do in this life—with one exception: Getting that dog of mine, Taffy, an English Setter, to pass Obedience Training school for the second time. Both times were utter failures. And now that I've used up all my allotted days, I might as well climb aboard and keep Byron company. Someone has to see to it that the ol' bird is taken care of properly and kept flying until the rest of the crew comes on board."
>
> The plane rolled to a stop and allowed her engines to idle. He turned around and jumped aboard. Paul was the second crewman to board Ol' Boomerang. He assumed his position between the two pilot seats. Then Ol' Boomerang revved up her engines, headed for the runway, and rose up quietly into the bright morning sunshine. With that said, Paul left us.

Paul, our good friend and B-24 crew chief, died at St. Agnes Hospital in Fresno, California. Only the hospital staff were in attendance at the time. A nurse came into the room to check on Paul and discovered that he had died. Paul's body was cremated and a memorial service was conducted in Los Angeles about four months after the death. Shirlene had put off major surgery for several months but was told by her doctor that she had to have the operation on Monday, November 8th. Flowers were sent to her by the crew members in a gesture of our concern for her well being and speedy recovery, and also in recognition of the loss of her husband and our esteemed flight crew engineer, Paul E. O'Steen.

Paul is survived by Shirlene, his third wife; two sisters; a brother; and a son, Paul E. O'Steen Jr., by his first wife; and two grandchildren, Mallory O'Steen, 4 1/2, and Renee O'Steen, 3 years old.

Sometimes for those left behind, the memory of the life of a friend or a family member is all too short. The memory of a person's existence lasts for only a couple of generations at the most. But for those whose lives he touched by his presence, the memories of his good humor, ready wit, loyalty to friends and family, and his dedication to duty—these character traits will last throughout eternity. It has been our good fortune to have known you, Paul; to have lived, worked, and flown in the big birds with you. In the past two years, we have had the pleasure of renewing our friendship with you, talking with you on many occasions. Your good natured smiling congeniality will be missed, but the memory of you always will remain with us.

Jim Snell, Top Turret Gunner
May 11, 1920–January 11, 1998

In the last ten days of his life, Jim knew that he was running out of time. He chose to do nothing about his medical problem and just wait quietly for Ol' Boomerang to show up. Now Ol' Boomerang's crew consists of Mike, Paul, Guy, Byron, and Jim.

Jim was born on May 11, 1920 in the remote area of Boon County, Missouri in a grocery store operated by his parents near the MK&T railroad stop. Jim was the second child born to Homer E. and Ora K. (Dodson) Snell. Eventually, the family grew to include five sisters and two brothers. Six children are alive at the present time. When Jim was three years old, the family moved to Harrisburg, Missouri and Jim started school at Duggan Elementary School. It housed eight grades. In 1927, the family moved to Columbia where Jim attended David Hickman High School and graduated in 1937. This was two years after the Japanese invaded China.

Immediately after graduation, Jim got a job with the County Bridge and Road Maintenance Department. Two months later, he went to work in a shoe factory. The family was beset with its first real tragedy on April 23, 1938. On that Saturday evening, Jim and a friend decided to take in a movie on Main Street in downtown Columbia. In front of Newberry's Department Store, Jim and his friend encountered Jim's father who was also in town on an errand. Jim's father asked him if he wanted to go with him to the store. But Jim answered, "No, Dad. I'll see you later at home." That was the last time Jim saw his father alive. After running his errand, Jim's father walked out into the street behind his parked car and did not see a fast approaching car. He was hit and killed. The driver of the car sped away but was apprehended shortly thereafter. This was the driver's second vehicular homicide in as many months.

After the movie, Jim and his friend encountered Jim's cousin in a restaurant and she told Jim that he had better get right home. There had been an accident. Jim decided to swing by the police station and inquire about the reported accident. The officer-in-charge said, "Oh yea, there was some guy by the name of Snell that got hit by a hit-and-run driver and was killed immediately.

"That was my father," Jim said, and returned home to be with his mother.

Shortly after his father's death, Jim met with his father's boss who asked him if he would like to apply for a job. Jim said yes and began working shortly thereafter. Jim's father had been employed by the Columbia City Light and Power plant. Jim obviously did succeed in his job as he retired from the power plant in 1980 as the Superintendent of the whole operation. An interesting side note is the fact that when Jim first began work, he was only a part-time employee with no employee benefits. He worked six days a week filling in for employees who had worked their 48-hour-shift schedules and needed time off. Jim's boss, Elrow Crane, must have been an interesting man because he told Jim the money he earned was to be given to his mother. But in fairness to Jim and his needs, Crane told Jim that he could work the seventh day and this day's pay was for Jim's use alone.

In 1938, Jim met Dorothy. At the time he was already working with Dorothy's father and they had become friends. In fact they trained pigeons together. A year later, July 31, 1939, Jim and Dorothy were married. Inasmuch as Jim had not had a day off since he started working at the plant, Jim decided to ask his boss if he could have one day off and chose not to tell why. His request was granted, but Jim suspected that the boss already knew of the importance of the request. Thereafter Jim and Dorothy lived in his mother's home until 1941 at which time Jim's mother remarried.

It wasn't until 1943 that the draft caught up with Jim. He was drafted into the service on August 20th and inducted at Ft. Leavenworth, Kansas. He took the GI. Intelligence test and was told that he could select any branch of the service he wished. Jim chose the Army Air Force. He also qualified for OCS and asked for pilot training school. Granted this request, the Army sent him to Sheppard Air Force Base in Wichita Falls, Texas. He sent for Dorothy and they spent four months there.

Jim recalled one test he took very vividly. He was summoned to the dispensary/infirmary building and asked by a medical officer if he would submit to a test. Jim said yes. With this, the officer produced a small glass pipette and told Jim to draw blood from his arm. Afterwards, Jim asked the officer why he had done this. The officer replied, "I just wanted to see if you would go through with the test." Reflecting on the incident, Jim wonders if it really had anything to do with God, Country, and Honor!

After completing basic training at Sheppard, Jim was sent to Stillwater, Oklahoma for Cadet Officer Training. Dorothy had come to both camps with Jim. Four months into his pilot training, the Army Air Corps was faced with a dilemma. How should it continue with its Officers Candidate School training program and still meet the demands for more and more air crews to man all the B-24s that were being produced by the thousands? Replacement crews were needed not only in the European Theater of Operations but also in the Pacific Theater. The war had to be brought to a successful conclusion as soon as was possible. To solve the problem, the Army decided to continue training only those cadets who had volunteered for service. The others would be sent to gunnery school and be assigned to crews for training in B-24s.

Jim's fate had been decided. He was sent to an Armament/Gunnery school in Laredo, Texas for four months of training. From here he was sent to Westover AFB. It was here that groups of 10 men were selected from a huge pool to form aircraft crews. Jim and the other nine members of the crew were sent to Charleston, South Carolina for overseas training. It was a very fortunate turn of events because Jim became a highly valued member of our crew. Jim was lucky enough to have Dorothy with him in Charleston where they lived in off-base housing. It was there that Dorothy met the wives of Roy and Bill. After the crew's training was completed, Dorothy followed Jim to New York. On arriving, Dorothy was told that she could be with Jim no longer for security reasons. She boarded another train and returned home.

Mitchell Air Force Base on Long Island, New York was an overseas assignment center where crews remained for only a few days. The crew was given its assignment and designated as the 13th replacement crew for the 514th Heavy Bombardment Squadron. On October 5, 1944, the crew and plane headed overseas via Newfoundland; the Portuguese Azores Islands; Morocco, Africa; Tunis, Tunisia; and finally San Pangrazio, Italy.

Seven missions into the crew's tour of duty, Jim was grounded because of an ear infection. At this time he asked for and received permission to visit his brother who was a corporal in the Army and stationed in Naples. On reaching his brother's encampment, he was treated like royalty by the other soldiers in his brother's outfit. After all, Jim was a Staff Sergeant and rank had its privileges. One morning, Jim and his brother encountered a Second Lieutenant, Jim's brother saluted the officer but Jim did not because it was not required in our Squadron during casual encounters. The officer did a "slow burn" because Jim did not show him the "proper respect due a Second Lieutenant," but he didn't say anything to Jim. Jim's brother and his tent mates were fearful of what the officer might do or say to them. However, nothing developed from the incident.

Jim, the ever quiet guy, went to San Pangrazio once a week to the home of a family that did washing for our crew. Jim gave the family unused bars of soap for which they were very grateful. Also, Jim frequently went to another town nearby, either Manduria or Lecce, where he ate and spent time with a family he befriended. After sharing meals with the family, he helped the 14-year-old daughter with her algebra homework. She knew very little English and Jim knew little or no Italian so it is not certain how much she learned.

After the crew returned states-side and the crew was disbanded in July 1945, Jim was assigned to an air base in Yuma, Arizona at a discharge processing center for returning airmen. He asked for a leave, went home, and returned with Dorothy. She remained with him until he was discharged from a base in San Bernardino, California early in November 1945.

Jim returned to his job at the power plant and began working his way back into the system. He also decided to sign up for some college courses in engineering. But as fate would have it, Jim's boss approached him with the offer of training that would lead to the position of Superintendent of the Power Plant. Jim accepted the offer and a college education was not considered again. He trained from 1948 to 1952 to handle any job connected with the running of the plant. Jim also took an ICS course and became the Assistant Superintendent in 1965. When offered the position of superintendent, Jim stepped aside in deference to a man who had seniority over him in order that the man could work a few years in that position until his retirement. Jim was also offered jobs in Jakarta and Guam but turned them down in deference to Dorothy.

Finally, Jim's time had come and he became the superintendent. He retired in June 1980.

Along the way Jim and Dorothy started their family. They had two sons, James E., born Sept. 11, 1948 and Kevin E., born August 10, 1952. Jim E. married Peggy. They have a stepson, Michael Lewis, now

21; daughter Kristen, age 16; and a son, James Aaron, age 14. James E. is chaplain in a correctional center. Kevin E., Jim's second son, is a business manager of the Columbia Public School System. He and his wife, Jo, have a step daughter, Traci, 23, and a son, Michael Shawn, age 23. He was always very proud of his family.

Dorothy was in ill health from the early 1980s until the time of her death in 1987. But Jim and Dorothy did manage to take a couple of trips during this time. The most memorable trip was to Niagara Falls in 1983.

In his retirement, Jim plays golf with a friend several times a week and looks forward to playing golf with his grandson, Michael Shawn, when he is in town. Of course there is a pool table in the basement for friends who care to take Jim on during bad weather days.

Michael Oczkus, Navigator
October 10, 1922–November 24, 1994

Mike is survived by his wife, Dorothy Hiber Oczkus; sons; Michael Gregory (Greg), Peter Bradford (Brad), David Stewart, daughter Lae-Helen Oczkus Stock, and son Mark Abel. The joy and the center of Mike's life in his later years were his grandchildren, Michael Stock, David Stock, Paul Stock, Peter Oczkus, Jonathan Oczkus, and Bryan Oczkus. Mike's parents were immigrants from Poland. They both were of Ukrainian heritage. Like so many other people of Eastern European descent, they had come to and saw America as the land of promise. They were young adults and did not know each other when they arrived in America. In fact, they first met in New York City. And it was there that they were married. Mike was the youngest of three sons and was raised in Brooklyn, New York. He was the last survivor of his parent's family, the others having died more than forty years ago.

Although little is known of Mike's early life prior to 1944, one short story will serve to point out his dedication to achieving an early-age goal that he had set for himself. Mike wished to enlist in the Army Air Corps when he was 18 years old, but his father wouldn't give Mike his approval and would not sign a consent form. So Mike did the next best thing, he signed up for a course in aircraft mechanics. By the time he had completed the course, he was old enough to enlist without his father's approval. Mike knew what branch of service and job he wanted to train. He wanted to join the Army Air Corps and to become a navigator. He talked about the following early military experience.

After finishing basic training, he applied for Officer Candidate School. The OCS test was easy and he was accepted but had to wait several months before his training as a navigator was to begin. He spent much of this time doing Kitchen Police (KP) duty week after week in a hot smelly kitchen wondering when this trial of his patience would end. Finally, a slot in the navigator's training school opened. He was on his way to becoming eventually one of the best navigators in the 514th Squadron—so was the belief of his crew and of other fellow officers. But Mike would never admit this truth to us or anyone else. There were other personal observations—bits and pieces of stories that he told Paul and myself in the fall of 1993 that gave us a better understanding of who Mike was. It was quite obvious that first and foremost, Mike was a dedicated family man. He also was an intellectual, a good mathematician, a religious man at heart, and a man of conviction and steadfast in his beliefs. He believed that deeds and actions had to match the principles by which one lived. These personal qualities were augmented by a dry and witty sense of humor that was constantly making itself evident when the opportunity was presented.

Mike was frequently flying with one crew or another in addition to those missions he flew with our crew. He finished up his 50-mission requirement before the rest of us and he wanted to get back states-side. Certainly his purpose was not to be retrained so that he could utilize his skills as a navigator on a B-29 flying over the Pacific Ocean. He had enough flying over a war zone and there was no point in tempting one's fate. So instead, he became a navigator for the Air Transport Command (ATC) navigating C-4s and C-47s, which gave him the opportunity to take in the sights of other interesting European countries.

An example of his dry, witty humor was when he spoke about the time he was absent without leave (AWOL) from the ATC. Referring to this blemish on his military record some 47 years later, he said with tongue in cheek, "I had never told anyone before that I was AWOL. But now that I have written this down, my conscience is clear. I feel better and I now can sleep nights."

A year and a half after flying for ATC, he sought and received a discharge from the Army Air Corps. He left for Anchorage, Alaska in 1946 where childhood Brooklyn friends had gone earlier and were awaiting his arrival and his participation in some type of a business opportunity. And what was that business? Mike and his close childhood friend, Al Kulis, bought a chicken hatchery. They raised and supplied Anchorage with the only fresh fryers available at the time. But this entrepreneurship was short-lived. The chicken processing plant burned down in 1948. Al dropped out of the partnership and Mike continued in the egg production business for several years thereafter.

Not only was Al Kulis Mike's childhood friend, but also they joined the service at the same time and went through OCS together. Al was a pilot during the war. After the war, Al had gone on to become a National Guard pilot stationed in Anchorage and was the first National Guard pilot to die in a crash. In his memory, the Air Force named an air base after him, Kulis Air Force Base.

But back to Mike, taking stock of his accomplishments and where he was, Mike thought it best to leave the job of raising chickens to other poultry farmers. In the intervening time, Mike's attention was diverted by a new and romantic interest, Dorothy Hiber. He married her during the month of July 1948. She was an employee of the Alaskan Rail Road (ARR). Coincidentally, she also was instrumental in getting him a job with the railroad in the winter of 1948.

Mike related the following story to Paul and me as he drove us to a local restaurant one morning to have breakfast. Mike gave a premier demonstration of his best wit in a very matter-of-fact manner with a straight-faced account of his first and last railroad experience. This was Mike at his very best as a story teller and humorist. Since Mike was good at working with his hands, the job with the railroad should have been a shoe-in, so to speak. He learned and completed his apprenticeship as a plumber and steam fitter and was given a job commensurate with his training. This trade became his lifelong work until he retired in 1984. However his tenure with the ARR was to be short-lived. Mike had become proficient enough in his trade to be entrusted with the training of another young man. Mike said, "One day I and my trainee were to do some repair work on a steam engine which was located on a piece of track that ended with a mechanical derailing device. During the repair, I told the trainee to make certain the brakes were set on the engine. But in the midst of his work, the trainee forgot. The engine began to move. There was no time to get back to the cab and set the brakes from where we were working. We jumped off the engine. The short and long of it was that the engine hit the derailer and flipped over. Well, at this point, I said to the trainee, 'I don't think there's any point of us going into the office and resigning, is there?' We both knew there was no future with the ARR, so we walked away from the scene and never returned." Both Paul and I laughed heartily at the end of his story.

It was in Anchorage that Mike and Dorothy became parents to four of their five children. As adults, Greg became an attorney practicing in Anchorage. Brad and David began working with Mike and learned his trade. Both are pipe and steamfitters working for the city of San Francisco. Lael Helen Oczkus Stock resides in Anchorage, and Mark is a businessman residing in El Cerrito, California.

The young family moved to Marin County, California in 1957. Mike and Dorothy bought a home in San Rafael in 1960, where they began raising their children.

Mike continued working in his chosen field, but things weren't going well for him in Local 38 of Plumbers' Union. Referring to the union, Dorothy said, "Mike took exception to the manner in which certain funds were being handled. He vociferously criticized the leadership, became unpopular, and he was forced to pay the price. He was blackballed by the union and couldn't get work." Knowing that his chances of getting a job in the area were nonexistent, he took on a job with Morrison & Knudsen as general foreman for the installation of water and steam pipelines working under contract to the Air Force. And where was this place of great opportunity? Vietnam, of course! The job was to provide the needed services for the building of Ton Son Hut Air Base. His stay there was the time when he became an avid letter writer telling the family of his many experiences—the good things, the bad things, the screw-ups, and the bombings, etc. His tour of duty in Viet Nam lasted two years from 1966 to 1968.

On returning home in 1968, he was still remembered for his criticism of the union and could not get work. As a result, he turned to the City of San Francisco where he worked until his retirement. One of the things that Mike was most proud of was the fact that he had supervised and installed much of the water sprinkling system for San Francisco's Golden State City Park located a few miles southeast of the Presidio and next to Point Lobos. His favorite spot was the rose garden located in front of the Arboretum. As painful as it may be for many modern American families, separation and divorce are a reality, and the Ozckus family was destined not to escape its grip. But the uniqueness of this family enabled it to overcome this scourge on family life. Because of the continuing commitment that Mike and Dorothy had to each other's well being as well as to that of their children, they developed and maintained a very special relationship, which continued to grow after their separation and the ultimate break up of their marriage. They were always there for each other in times of need. Neither of them remarried. When Mike developed a serious heart problem, in the mid 80's, followed by the need for surgery, Dorothy spent two months helping him to accept, adjust, and regain a limited life style. He traveled to Cottage Grove, Oregon (her home) at least four times since 1991. Mike went there for the last time in September 1993. This time he supervised the improvement of the heating system and involved himself in various other home projects.

In many families, the children can't wait until they grow up and to leave home. The opposite was true in Mike's family. The children didn't want to leave home after graduating from high school. Mike continued to live in his San Rafael home until his death but he never was really left alone. His children and grandchildren were constantly popping in on him or he would go to their homes and enjoy their company. And of course there was the swimming pool to take advantage when visiting. Mike's children and grandchildren were always to remain the real source of his pride and enjoyment.

Dorothy said, "In the later years of his life, the best thing for him was having all or some of his children and their families over to his house for sumptuous dinners. He was most happy when his children were around. And he adored the grandsons as witnessed by the hallway walls of his house covered with their pictures. Mike's final request was that he be cremated, leaving behind instructions to his children to choose the place to scatter his ashes. They chose the Rose Garden of Golden Sate Park, which was one of his favorite places. Of course this choice was not strictly legal, but I know Mike would not let that stop him if he were making the choice. Mike's final request was that there should be no funeral after he died, so his children planned an event to celebrate his wake and life at his home. It was attended by several generations of neighbors, school friends of his children and even some of their parents, relatives of his daughters-in-law, and some people who may have never been inside his house before but who wanted to pay their respects for the neighborliness he had shown them. It was a wonderful party."

Mike was also one of those individuals who was not concerned about the outward appearances of thing, be they what he wore, the rock garden in front of his house, or the garage that had taken on the 32-year collection of everything from his daughter's small sports car and boat to those things that he was sure he had to save because they might come in handy some day. Dorothy says, "Mike's garage is and always has been a disaster area."

In the finest sense of the term, Mike was a diamond in the rough and a true friend to those who had earned his respect.

Finally, Mike's ability to write has left us with much material providing us with laughs, humor, wit, and insights. He sent me 32 hand-written pages describing his military experiences and anecdotal stories not only for our entertainment and amusement, but also as a legacy to his children and their children. Mike also wrote over 20 pages that were private and meant only for his family.

Paul and I first discovered his flair for writing during our visit in August 1992. During a Friday evening bull session, Mike modestly asked if I would like to read a few pages of something that he had written. When I said yes, he went to his bedroom and returned with six handwritten pages. Both Paul and I read them and we were quite astonished at his ability to express himself so very well as a narrator and humorist. I asked him for more of his written thoughts. He appeared to be very pleased and said no more about the subject. That was all the motivation Mike needed to really start cranking out what had been stored away in his brain for 47 years. I believe he really did enjoy writing his memories, thoughts, and stories for family and crew. Reflecting on our whole crews coming together for a brief period of time, Dorothy said, "You men coming back into his life was one of the best things that every happened to him."

On November 24th, the day before Thanksgiving, Mike's pen lay silent. No more stories to be told. He had just returned home from the grocery store lugging a 20-pound turkey only a few minutes before. He had known the moment of truth was upon him when he said to himself, "I'll just lie down and rest a bit."

> In the twilight of his life, Mike rose up and put on his old flying suit, officer's hat, and the well-worn, brown leather flight jacket with the individual silver bars painted on the epaulets. He picked up his sextant and E-6B navigational calculator knowing there was one

last mission to fly. Ol' Boomerang was approaching once again, this time to pick up Mike. It was as if Boomerang also knew that there was a third mission to fly in the ebbing light of this day. Paul and Byron were both on board now, so, quietly, Ol' Boomerang circled, landed, and waited for Mike to come aboard. In the manner of his youth, he ducked under the opened bomb bay and jumped up and onto the catwalk leading to the flight deck. He chatted a bit with Paul and Byron and then he turned and made his way through the crawl space under the flight deck towards his navigator's table located in the open space to the left and just behind the nose turret. Once again ready to chart an unchartered course.

Michael Oczkus, may you fly with the wind to your back, navigate a true course, and fly into everlasting sunlight.

0-595-34738-X

Printed in the United States
86216LV00004B/162/A